Global praise for Diary of a Former Covidiot

"Witty, clever and addictive, I recognised myself and others in the hilarious stories Christina Thé brings us in *Diary of a Former Covidiot*! A timely, light-hearted record of crazy behaviour against the backdrop of a pandemic that has rocked the world in our lifetime.

Christina Thé brings the reader stories from her own world in Singapore, introducing hilarious characters doing crazy things. We will recognise Covidiot behaviour in ourselves and those around us whilst trying to 'survive the pandemic', making us nod along and laugh out loud.

Whilst acknowledging the grief that COVID-19 has caused many, Christina seeks to offer some light relief from the situation, recording this new, strange way of life.

This book is a timely page turner and makes a great gift that can be dipped into over again. Read it and share it — will bring a much needed laugh to many!"

—Eleanor O'Connor
Penguin Random House Publishing, UK

"Funny as hell. It's comedy gold. Thoroughly entertaining from first to last page. Christina Thé wittily takes the reader on the roller coaster ride that is the pandemic, from a satirical and comically honest perspective. Pages are filled with light-hearted humour and satisfying laugh-out-loud moments. I really enjoyed this book!"

—Clarissa Santoso
PhD Student, USA

"FF'rickin hilarious and screenplay-worthy! You ROCK, The Christina Thé!"

—Ben Chan
Executive Producer, Red Compass Media, Inc., USA

"Finally a book not only so relatable but a massive comic relief that reflects the e   ore COVID/ During COVID)   nk you, it's a godsend for my s   ing this book while sipping G8

-Ethel Reyes
Medical Scientist, Australia

"This should be standup comedy material."

—**Andre Surya**
Civil Engineer, Indonesia

"Very funny. Especially the chapter, *About Hair*. The big hair episode with her aunts amused me very much! A nice glimpse of how contrasting cultures react to the same situation, the pandemic. Light hearted and presented in a very fun way, Christina's way :)"

—**Jeong Ae Ree**
Artistic Director of New Opera Singapore

"A brilliant storyteller."

—**Shanti Bhattacharya**
Heritage Guide, Singapore

"What an amazing sense of humour! Hilarious and funny insight into people's behavior — clever observation into life in the supermarket jungle! To me the most touching part of the book is when the sisters say they love each other (in the story, *Motherhood is the greatest job you'll ever fxxx up*). So simple but huge impact. Well done."

—**Peter Ng**
Entrepeneur, Simgapore

"Extremely entertaining and relaxing to read! I am a senior European lady, yet I still find the stories very engaging. This optimistic book is a breath of fresh air. It is just what we all need right now!"

—**J.N.**
Retired Principal Mezzo-Soprano of Opera Australia

"Very witty. I like it a lot, especially the part with the aunts doing their hair. I can clearly picture them!"

—**Christina Hindle**
Fellow Mum, Austria

"Witty and original! Love it! And, LMAO... the plot twists!"

—**Alfani Cahya**
Fulltime Mum of Two, Indonesia

DIARY OF A FORMER COVIDIOT

Tales of Panic Buying,

Surviving and Finding Humour

during the Coronavirus Pandemic

Christina Thé

Marshall Cavendish
Editions

Published by Marshall Cavendish Editions
An imprint of Marshall Cavendish International

A member of the
Times Publishing Group

Other Marshall Cavendish Offices:
Marshall Cavendish Corporation, 800 Westchester Ave, Suite N-641, Rye Brook, NY 10573, USA • Marshall Cavendish International (Thailand) Co Ltd, 253 Asoke, 16th Floor, Sukhumvit 21 Road, Klongtoey Nua, Wattana, Bangkok 10110, Thailand • Marshall Cavendish (Malaysia) Sdn Bhd, Times Subang, Lot 46, Subang Hi-Tech Industrial Park, Batu Tiga, 40000 Shah Alam, Selangor Darul Ehsan, Malaysia

Marshall Cavendish is a registered trademark of Times Publishing Limited

National Library Board, Singapore Cataloguing in Publication Data

Name(s): Thé, Christina.
Title: Diary of a former covidiot : tales of panic buying, surviving and finding humour during the coronavirus pandemic / Christina Thé.Description: Singapore : Marshall Cavendish Editions, [2020]
Identifier(s): OCN 1158579586 | ISBN 978-981-4893-78-7 (paperback)
Subject(s): LCSH: COVID-19 (Disease)--Social aspects--Fiction. | Epidemics--Fiction.
Classification: DDC S823--dc23

Printed in Singapore

Publisher's Note: All characters and incidents mentioned in this book are fictional and based entirely on the author's imagination. Any similarities to persons, dead or alive, are coincidental.

For Felix Cheong

Writer, Mentor, Friend and Covidol

A COVIDIOT'S COMMANDMENTS

"Thou Shall Not Be A Covidiot."

"Thou Shall Not Covid Thy Neighbour."

"Thou Shall Stay At Home."

COVIDIOT [*Noun, informal*]

Definitions and synonyms

Someone who continues to go out and socialise
despite being told repeatedly to stay at home;

A person who hoards goods (especially toilet paper,
masks and sanitisers), denying them from their neighbours;

A person who does not observe social distancing;

Someone who does not wear a mask when outside
or in contact with the general public;

Someone who goes immediately to the supermarket
in anticipation of the Prime Minister's address;

Someone who ill-treats or evicts front-line
medical heroes out of their rental properties,
or park at doctors' and nurses' parking lots in hospitals.

Someone who touches others without sanitising their hands,
or simply, touches or hugs others in this day and age.

INTRODUCTION

> "*When the storm breaks, each man acts in accordance with his own nature. Some are dumb with terror. Some flee. Some hide. And some... spread their wings like eagles and soar on the wind.*"
> — Dr John Dee (1527–1608), mathematician.

———

Be it on my faraway travels or around my neighbourhood, I have always loved observing human nature and behaviour—both on and off the stage.

I find human beings most intriguing. We are complex, resilient, adaptable, yet at times, comical.

At this current moment, nothing is more interesting than observing human behaviour during this global pandemic of unprecedented scale. Those who survive, truly are living a part of history.

What I also found is that even the most dire of situations can be inundated with precious, humorous moments.

The earlier stories in the book were written with the sole purpose to bring a smile to family and friends who are dear to me, in different parts of the world. With so much doom and gloom and negativity that besieged us, I wished to present a light-hearted contrast to lift up their spirits.

My little vignettes unexpectedly became an extended account that was conceived entirely during the global lockdown—a happy yet near impossible feat.

Singing a line of lyrics is not the same as writing a line of text as I soon discovered. Especially while educating and keeping alive my two favourite little humans at home. I am sure it's an experience some of you can relate to.

The book is grouped according to themes around the events of the Coronavirus pandemic. Each chapter is a standalone tale. You can flip to any chapter randomly and not have missed the plot. Packed in manageable bite-sized pieces. Nothing too mentally taxing.

I hereby present to you, stories of challenges and human resilience, of herd mentality and overcoming fear, as seen from a humorous perspective. This is a work of observational fiction inspired by true events and real characters, written with lots of dramatic licence. It may seem like a narrative of others' experiences, but truly, these are our stories together.

Let us always look up and brave adversity with a smile. To those who lost your loved ones to this pandemic, we are united in your grief.

The facts of our predicament may remain the same, but we have a choice to observe the amusing side of things, or to let our spirits be reduced by circumstances. It is a choice we make every day, wherever we are in the world.

On another note, most of us might have been a Covidiot at some point or another, some more so than others. Here's a cheeky reminder to finally be reborn a Covidol! What could be more appropriate than an account written by a singing (and former) Covidiot.

I hope these short stories remind you of something, or someone. Above all, I hope they bring some light to your day and a smile to your face, as they did to those near and dear to me.

Let us begin.

ON FAMILY & PANIC BUYING

On Family Distancing

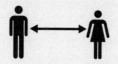

It's interesting to observe how people's strategies differ with regards to this Coronavirus (or COVID-19 which is its hip name now).

One extreme example is my dear dad.

He's barricaded himself for the past month or so in his apartment unit. Along with his wife this time, unlike that Swine/Bird Flu episode some years back when he told mum and I that we were to quarantine ourselves for a few days at Le Meridien upon landing at Changi Airport before we were allowed to come home to our flat in Singapore (yes, they're still married now).

Dad rang me some weekends ago with what he thought was a piece of the worst news ever: the Catholic Church had ceased Masses, indefinitely.

Side Note: Ever since my divorce, dad's gone completely religious and attends Mass once a day. Maybe… if I had brought home that bejewelled hip-hop star I became acquainted with at the F1 race and said, "Dad, meet your new son-in-law," he would have given the religious fanatics a run for their money and prayed in church six times a day. Well, people have different coping mechanisms, whatever works.

I feigned the best imitation of a grunt to convey sympathy at his predicament whilst at the same time texting my Korean BFF saying, "We no go church tomorrow." (followed by five happy emoticons).

Last weekend there was an exodus of fleeing cousins from Jakarta, just in time before the lockdown. He was as terrified of catching things from them as they are of him (just him, per se, not the virus). I was supposed to keep things hush-hush from the parents so he was not supposed to know this, but apparently I underestimated his old people WhatsApp group.

A message typed in capital letters came in, "DON'T SEE YOUR COUSINS! THEY'RE HERE!"

The other Sunday night he dropped off my girls, wearing a mask, in his car. When I knocked on the glass window, he refused to wind down the window. Instead, I got a wave. Never seen him drove faster in my life (for a man who drives 20km/h if he could have his way, he was going at a Maclaren speed off a curb).

Last week, before shit hit the fan globally, I tried to calm dad down and copied and pasted a text message from a dear friend. The message said that more people died from traffic accidents in a year than from the virus. Dad was not amused. My friend said not to tell dad that the information was from him.

Funny how as I am laughing at him now, fancying myself super chill, here I am yelling at my kids who just came home from school: "DON'T TOUCH YOUR FACE!!" armed with Dettol hand sanitiser and spraying all around, the liquid narrowly missing their eyes.

Love my dad. I guess we're not so different after all.

The Quest for a Hen

"Men! MEN! So many men! Men everywhere! Oooo... I am so stressed! I have never seen these many men! Men took ALL my toilet paper! BLA BLA BLA BLA BLA..." my mum proclaimed.

It suddenly become apparent to me where my propensity for theatrics came from.

Interestingly, dad thought her most ravishing in her 20s when she managed to wake the whole village by shouting everywhere that there was a fire in her brother's kitchen. The villagers doused it off, and my dad and her got married.

She, along with the horde of panic buyers, descended upon the supermarkets in Singapore when they heard the news that Malaysia had closed its borders.

I replied carelessly, "Oh... good. Can meet new man there."

My mum responded, "How can you find a new boyfriend there? I had to wrestle a cabbage from a man just now! They are not interested in women! They want FOOD! Toilet paper!"

Why she did not tell me earlier about these men in supermarkets. I did not know supermarkets were the best venue to meet men these days. I could have assisted her, or them.

She said she went to three supermarkets; ranging from cheap to expensive. She found many, many men there. To her dismay, and mine too (because I did not meet them).

Mum lamented, "Your father wanted to eat *temulawak* (an Indonesian root vegetable believed to ward off COVID-19). I brought a lot of money as needed to buy a lot. But no *temulawak*! Got money also cannot buy! Ahhhh, must pray to God that this virus stops soon! Ahhhh, I'm so stressed!"

Earlier in the week my iphone X fell onto my foot at a funny angle whilst I was trying to hit high notes on the piano for my new opera. Freak accident. It must have been fractured. I told Mum I could not walk very well but if she had told me about this phenomenon, I could have had a miraculous recovery.

I said even more carelessly, "Mum, I think we need to rear our own chickens from now on. For eggs. Tell dad to buy. I only know where to buy hamsters. Make sure it's female ah, hens."

I texted my brother to ask if we needed a cock to make a hen lay eggs. I must have slept throughout that part of Biology class. He did not bother replying. Maybe he was asleep during the class too.

I started eyeing my little girls' toy potted plant kits that proclaimed on the boxes, "Grow a strawberry" or "Grow a tomato" thinking maybe this could be an alternative source of food. If my dad could get the live chicken somehow, and I grow these plants somewhere on the condominium grounds (by the way, it's not allowed), maybe we'll survive the apocalypse. As we did SARS, Donald Trump and so many other atrocities.

Talk to you lovely folks later. Need to go find a mama hen now.

In a supermarket.

An Oriental Discovery

DISCLAIMER: To be read with a GIGANTIC sense of humour!

* * *

A recent after-school conversation I had with my eldest girl, Sophia, reminded me of an encounter I had in the UK.

TIMELINE: INDEFINITE YEARS AGO
Once upon a time, I went on a road trip to the English countryside with a kindly British companion. I had not expected to meet so many people who look like me on this trip. Three whole, loud, busloads of them.

My companion quickly ushered me away, as if to protect me, to another corner of the tourist town whispering, "Let's avoid the Chinese."

I looked up at him. There was no other direction for a midget like me but to look up considering the man was 6 feet 4 inches tall. We must have looked like a pairing of a St. Bernard and a Chihuahua. I guess to each his own...

I laughed my head off, pointed at myself, enunciating every word, "But, you have YOUR very own Chinese here."

"Yes. But you know, you're not 'that' kind of Chinese."

I decided not to point out that whatever he was wearing was probably China-made from head to toe, including his camera.

We looked over and at a glance saw 60 selfie-sticks up in the air with a sea of compulsory index and middle fingers ready for photos. For some reason I was convinced they were a healthy combination of all yellows imaginable, i.e. Chinese, Koreans, Japanese, Taiwanese, etc. But, just because we are all yellow doesn't necessarily mean we always get along. The Koreans are in agreement though, when it comes to the Japanese, whilst Taiwan and China are... well, you know.

Me (resolutely): "They are not Chinese. I'll prove it to you. Let's go over and eavesdrop."

We didn't have anything better to do anyway so I dragged the gentle giant over to the tourist groups. I noticed some of them had started leaving their single use plastic bottles everywhere. Bad. Bad.

Presently, I heard my mother's Javanese dialect spoken.

They were Indonesians.

* * *

TIMELINE: TODAY

Setting: At the dining table, late afternoon. The kids are doing their homework. Me, eating *kerupuk* (Asian crackers).

Sophia: "Mum, today I played with Isae (a lovely French girl who is her BFF) and a new boy in school. He does not speak English. I used sign language to communicate with him. Nobody played with him. He was alone."

Me (perked up, munching vigorously): "Oh? Who is this new friend? That's really nice of you. I'm so proud of you my Sophiakins. Yes, all of us were once a new kid in school right, Mummy is proud of you, you've done the right thing. You know when I was a kid too... blah blah blah."

Smug and proud, I tooted my own inner horn of how well I've brought up my little girl. So I just posted a good samaritan Goalcast clip on social media about the importance of extending our hand in friendship at school to everyone, especially to those with special circumstances.

Sophia: "His name is...." (two-syllable Oriental name).

Me (frozen with mouth agape as the horror set in) : "Oh, did he just arrive? How long ago?"

Sophia: "A few months ago."

Me (barely moving): "Really? Months or weeks? Did he go back to his hometown between then and now?"

Sophia (9 years old, looking up at me irritably, muttering flatly): "Mum. He does not have Coronavirus."

* * *

Shame, shame, for shame Christina.

[Soundtrack: Avenue Q the Musical's *Everyone's a Little Bit Racist* blaring in the background].

Turmeric Will Save Us All

"We eat Indian," my dad decreed, upon his discovery that there was no Coronavirus in India (at that time). "The Indians got it right. Simon says they are ok because of their food. We just follow. From now on we'll just eat Indian food."

This was before Coronavirus was granted its royal title, Covid the 19th, and before every country (including India) had a visit from this royal nightmare of a virus.

Simon is my dad's long-time friend of over 20 years. They met after our unceremonious relocation to Singapore. He is Indian and he looks to us to weigh more than the average scale limits, with a sense of humour to match. He's on a first name basis with the whole length of Race Course Road's food establishments.

My Dad, instead, is a health freak.

You know when the vitamin shop sales people bow Japanese style to you upon your exit out of their shop, you probably have purchased more nutrients than you ought to. He eats brown rice (I never could come to terms with this), and exercises 5x a week. Enough said.

Quite an odd looking couple they are, with a robust friendship.

I challenged dad vehemently saying that's what Indonesian officials said too. They and their root vegetable. They claimed there were no Coronavirus cases in Indonesia, and when they were politely questioned by the World Health Organsation (WHO) of their suspiciously placid situation, they wrote an angry letter back to WHO. See whose pants are on fire now, with citizens fleeing (or dropping) right and left.

Now it's been a while since my dad ate outside food. "Don't know who has coughed on it," he said.

My brother, who loves all food Western, meekly protested, "We are not Indian. How do we know how to cook Indian food? I don't even know where to start."

My dad, "Super simple lah. Google. You find recipe. You print. Give to the helper."

I offered to ask Indian friends for tips which I reckoned would be immensely more authentic than the internet but dad preferred Chef Google.

My good fortune in terms of domestic gastronomy in this instance was notable, seeing as I do not live at the same address as my folks.

For the next three days they ate their own version of Indian food. For breakfast, lunch and dinner.

My brother reported it was basically turmeric and masala plus chicken. He would not have minded it if it's from a proper Indian restaurant but what he had did not resemble any Indian food we've ever had. He said if he ate any more turmeric he was going to turn yellow from head to toe.

I don't know how that's going to happen seeing as my very light-yellow skinned brother, bless him, with slits as eyes, cannot look more yellow than he already is. But life is full of surprises. Like that time the ICA (Immigration and Checkpoints Authority) officer gruffly asked him to prove he was of Chinese descent as he wrote he was, before they approved his PR (permanent resident) permit extension.

I visited the family home unannounced the other day.

Upon entering the main hallway I caught sight of a figure surreptitiously making a dash from the back door going in the direction of the bedrooms. I thought, "OMG! It's a thief! OMG, OMG, OMG!"

In the absence of any weapon, and as I was trapped in there anyway, I prepared myself to do what I am classically trained best to do: scream.

As I took a deep breath, mouth agape, my brother jumped from the hallway and motioned for me to shut up.

He said, "Pssstttt! Come into my room and I'll share my loot."

There in the centre of the room was the biggest gourmet burger I'd ever seen. The poor sod was desperate for his usual sane food.

It took us back to our childhood when we were both complicit in doing something illegal. We ate and we giggled, two old rats we were. My brother finished his share of the burger in five minutes. Dad was nowhere to be seen, probably taking a nap, or so we thought. I'm pretty sure I heard him snore.

Until the door opened unexpectedly. It swung open while I was putting that last bit of onion into my mouth. One, caught.

[Curtain. Exeunt.]

The Supermarket: A Modern Jungle

The plot thickens on a recent phenomenon of men found all over supermarkets (see Chapter 2).

It was generally agreed at this stage that COVID-19 sucks. It mucks up the order of things on so many levels. If we were fortunate enough to still be alive at all.

Take grocery shopping for example which has become a new dilemma for every family.

Out of the members of each household, someone needs to be appointed as the chosen one, i.e. a 'sacrificial tribute' to go out and brave the virus outside in order to buy the essentials.

Of late it seemed that more and more men were taking one for the team and reverted to their original role of being the hunter; as befitted their role as head and protector of the family.

Except for one tiny little glitch.... the modern 'jungle' has evolved. In Singapore, it is called NTUC Fairprice, i.e. an affordable supermarket chain meant for peasants (like me).

This created a whole new set of problems of men being tasked to buy a specific list of items, and coming back with a bunch of something else entirely different.

This week I found myself as the default patsy in my family to join the mob in my neighbourhood NTUC, and witnessed for myself this sudden phenomenon.

Why me? (Yes, why me...) Well, the parents were too old and too scared; the kids were too young: the domestic helper was too indispensable; and the brother? He once brought home zucchini instead of cucumber. Not the ideal Tribute.

Channeling *Hunger Games'* Katniss Everdeen, heroically armed with mask and one gallon of sanitiser, I headed over to the jungle. Now you may think this is a lot of liquid but trust me I finished it all before I stepped back through my front door. It's amazing that I haven't had sanitiser poisoning yet.

I scanned the crowd. The ratio of men to women in each aisle was 4:1. The few scattered ladies I spotted went about their business knowing exactly what to grab with Olympic-like speed and accuracy. Sharp. With shark-like strides they hunted. Such Amazons.

They were a stark contrast to the obviously married men. Each was carrying a shopping list, which from their expressions, might as well be written in hieroglyphs.

They were confused.

Some walked around in circles in the aisles. Some walked up and down the aisle from one end to the other, and back again as if it were a runway. Some were seen on a loop pattern amongst several aisles, like a circle line train, appearing and reappearing at the same spot again. Some were just really, really lost.

Some were looking for that ONE elusive, horror item.

I would guess that elusive item was sanitary napkins, guessing from the masculine crowd forming a messy horizontal line, scanning up and down the party wares section under 'napkins'.

On this note I encountered my neighbour contemplating a row of items, with the word Durex emblazoned on the display rack. I guess people have different priorities during a lockdown.

When I chanced upon him, he was clearly startled and to save face, quickly jumped one step to the next rack. Unfortunately for him, this was where the real sanitary napkins were; which the rest of his confused comrades were looking for.

That rack's order from left to right:
Sanitary Napkins — Birth Control — Infant Formula
Success — Prevention — Fail

The irony.

I walked on and with a chuckle overheard a gentleman on speakerphone. I presumed from the highly irritated tone that it must have been his wife on the line, "I said mung beans, not long beans. Yesterday you brought back French beans! Aiyoh, I told you, just look at the labels below the products. You go ask the staff which aisle." (Yes, men would absolutely ask for directions... Not.)

"Dear, beans are beans lah. They are all green what. Why so many kinds of beans?" In his defence, mung beans in Malay is 'kacang hijau' which translates as green beans.

Another man had his phone on hands-free mode and it was clear that he had a slightly more understanding wife. He turned left, paused, took three steps forward, paused, one step back, looked right, paused again to listen to instructions, and took an item from the second shelf from the top. It was a blue packet and he carefully read aloud the label before depositing it with a flourish into the shopping trolley with a triumphant look on his face. And off he crashed into another confused married man.

My last pit stop was the eggs section. I haven't had much success securing a live hen to lay eggs in my condo. I asked a friend if he would chaperone me to go look for live chickens in Singapore and he said it would be dangerous. I asked for whom? He said, for both the chicken and us. I guess the thought of a plucky chicken in the back seat of his mother's Mercedes was not quite ideal.

Here, a man was contemplating the many choices of eggs: omega, free-range, kampong, grain-fed, probiotics, etc. How can anyone not be confused? Even I was confused.

I whispered to him with a smile, "Keep it simple. Grab and run. They're all eggs."

A Family Affair

This unfortunate pandemic brings out interesting aspects of everyone's family dynamics. It certainly did for the senior members of my family.

My maternal grandparents had nine children. Boy, girl, boy, girl, in an almost perfect two-year interval between each birth (except for the happy surprise in the end, my ninth aunt who is not that much older than my eldest cousin). My mum at number six is somewhere in the middle.

I have steadfastly declined to be part of this extended family's WhatsApp group. I knew that for better or for worse, it would not stop beeping, what with nearly 20 retirees exchanging information and contrasting opinions on all topics imaginable: from detergent and grandchildren, to melatonin and the Pope. I had somehow managed to elude the group and just appreciate family news and gossips from afar.

The occurrence of the Coronavirus has caused the activity in the Elders WhatsApp Group (EWG) to spike up to a whole new level.

The elders were all in a panic, understandably so, seeing as they fit the bill perfectly as the typical Coronavirus newspaper headliners. They were all in their 70s or pushing 70, other than their youngest sibling. It did not help that some of their friends of similar age had become statistics, too.

Here are some members of the EWG.

Eldest auntie (child no. 2): A former soprano and a finalist of the national classical singing competition of Indonesia's national radio in her youth. She became a professional, renowned *wayang* (Indonesian-Malay traditional opera) artist in Central Java, with hair three metres long in her heyday. Legend has it that two people were required to help wash her hair manually using pails of water. Yes, Rapunzel did exist. It's cropped short now. She was allegedly my grandfather's favourite daughter, until my Mum took over. Will refer to her as Soprano Auntie.

Second uncle (child no. 3): A doctor by profession, he's charitable, calm, very funny in an intellectual way and was universally acknowledged to be very smart. He's on TV and on social media everywhere now (voluntarily so) giving guidance to the public on how to avoid getting COVID-19. He was particularly known for his innovative demonstration on how to wear a mask properly. He cheekily admitted that he used to snatch my second auntie's share of egg during meals in their childhood. He claimed that she ate very slowly. Interestingly, he grew up tall while she did not. Let's call him Doctor Uncle for this story.

My mum (child no. 6): Vivacious and artistic, yet politically correct. She mentors her church youth choir group. Now she's very free, as her grandchildren are locked away at my house and the choir is shut. Default hairdresser to my Dad at home. She has a booming voice that carries. Sounds familiar?

Second auntie (child no. 4): A very gentle, wisp of a person with a serene smile. Petite lady with immeasurable quiet wisdom and is kindness personified. Seems to be quite frail but somehow always the one who outlasts everybody else. She is my Gentle Auntie.

Husband of second auntie above: a jovial, very helpful, fit gentleman, sociable and just an easy going chap all around.

Third uncle (he's no. 7, just after my mum): A retiree with hypochondriac tendencies and general anxiety issues. Otherwise for all appearances, he is a very fit, good-looking man with a generous personality.

Wife of youngest uncle (her husband is no. 8): No. 8 was a planned child before the final surprise and he was allegedly my grandmother's favourite. He was famously born in a rickshaw on the way to the hospital. My humorous, young-at-heart, aunt-in-law lives in the Philippines with my retired uncle. He has a hilarious sense of humour but was not currently participating in the Coronavirus discussion at the EWG.

Of late, the elders have been so terrified of the virus that they won't even open their windows for fear of it somehow flying in as they live in landed houses in the suburbs.

A snippet of their recent conversation:

Soprano Auntie: "Yes lah. I am already very stressed."

Mum: "Take a deep breath *jie* (older sister in Mandarin). Try and sing karaoke. You'll feel better. I bought myself a new microphone."

Doctor Uncle (interjecting): "Ah, she's always stressed. Even if can go outside the house."

P.S. In case you still cannot tell by now, my mum's family is a family of singers/musicians/artists. We never needed to hire a choir for family weddings. It's always the family who provided the choir and soloists. Whoever married into it by default will sing in the choir too (or pretend to sing). Each occasion was an anecdote in itself, with these siblings taking jibes at one another during rehearsals. Comments could include, "Haha, *kor*, you sang flat today," while the accused retorts, "I most certainly was not flat. I never sing flat. You sang too loud." And so on.

Soprano Auntie: "I tried. I opened my mouth inside my house and tried to sing. Eh. The sound came out flat because I'm too stressed. My voice cannot come out."

My Mum: "Hahaha." She laughed a little too happily.

My Eldest Aunt singing flat was as absurd as it could be. She was supposed to the diva amongst the siblings.

Gentle Auntie: "*Jie*, try and drink hot green tea."

Husband of Gentle Auntie: "Try foot reflexology."

Another Uncle: "Hot shower, not cold shower. Later you will catch wind (a traditional term for the general state of being unwell)."

Then there were suggestions flying around in the chat group from my Doctor Uncle that Soprano Auntie's son do foot reflexology for his widowed mother instead of going *pak tor* (dating) with his girlfriend, or at least a shoulder massage, a service which he said he has dutifully performed.

Third Uncle (not the doctor) fretfully declared: "No, no, no. At this time, no singing. It's very dangerous. We should not open our mouths at all cost. Even at home, I wear a mask, you know. Cannot take chances! You don't know if the virus happens to be flying around the house."

My mum: "Aiyah, at home is ok lah. Can open mouth. Otherwise how to eat??"

Third Uncle: "This is what we all should do. Keep the mouth closed, wear mask and gargle with salt water for an hour, three times a day."

Gentle Auntie: "Why?"

Third Uncle: "The point is we should keep our mouths shut at all times. Singing can cause sore throat. See, you open your mouth too long you'll get sore throat."

More comments and objections flying around.

Third Uncle (still pressing on with his manifesto): "I wear a mask even when I sleep! At home we must still wash hands every 30 minutes!"

Another Uncle sniggering: "Hohoho, this is a very good time to pick a fight with my wife. She cannot talk back."

Doctor Uncle: "Stress is a choice. Happiness is also choice."

Wife of Youngest Uncle: "What about when eating? Where should I put my husband? Should I keep him two metres away? Or should we take turns wearing masks while the other eats?"

Third Uncle (missing the point): "Can eat a lot. Must eat a lot. Sleep must use mask. Eh, don't laugh ah, ask *kor kor*, he's also wearing." Referring to Doctor Uncle who now promotes masks night and day all over the media.

"I already told our big brother that according to our family's genetics, we all needed to wear masks when sleeping, especially for us. For you (addressing his youngest sister-in-law), maybe no need, because different genes," he carried on.

A cousin suddenly remarked: "Why the preferential treatment, uncle?"

Third Uncle preached solemnly: "Happy are those who can sleep without masks. You see, our whole family sleeps with our mouths open. It's terrible! Always got sore throat! Very, very dangerous."

My mum: "Maybe it's just you. I don't sleep with my mouth open."

Husband of Gentle Auntie (referring also to youngest sister-in-law): "But don't forget to remove mask when showering."

Third Uncle (in a state): "I research! Everyday I research. I read, and I read, and I read on the internet, which country, which place in the world can we go to avoid this bloody Coronavirus. Which city does not have this virus. At first I thought New Zealand. It's far enough. *Alamak*, they also *kena* (loosely translated as affected in this context)! How? So stressed. Where can we go?"

Soprano Auntie (clearly not paying heed to her younger brother's rant, was still stuck on the earlier topic, and apparently had been busy vocalising): "I can sing now."

Third Uncle (also not paying attention to his eldest sister): "Ah! You know, I found it! I found the perfect place where we all can move to. It's Timor Leste! Zero case! I am going to move there," he boomed resolutely. (FYI: Timor Leste is a small, young nation situated in the Indonesian archipelago, and for lack of a better word, rather natural. It's basically an outback).

Protests erupted. First in line amongst the protestors was Third Uncle's own wife, who suddenly came to life on the chat group.

This spirited discussion on my Third Uncle's proposed grand plan of our extended family's exodus to Timor Leste continued for a good part of the week as I was told by my cousins, the silent audience.

Hey, you'll never know, maybe remote island living is the solution. But I'm already on my favourite island and I'm staying put, for better or worse.

About Hair

The phone rang very close to midnight. It was my mum. We were all night owls but I thought this was rather alarming. These days people only call when it's an emergency, right? I thought somebody had died.

She said, "My sisters are coming here next week. Go find a hairdresser for them. No, not that one you found for me before. He's terrible, cannot make big hair. Find somebody who can comb properly otherwise your Auntie Mei won't be happy."

By 'comb', my mum meant those big, backcombed hair of her generation. Some call it helmet hair, some call it a beehive, in Singapore they call it *ibu* hair ('ibu' pronounced 'ee-boo', literally means 'mother' or 'madam' in Indonesian).

Those who are younger may not know but there is a whole group of ladies from our parents' generation who go to a salon to wash their hair and get it styled every week. Some of them have not washed their own hair at home for the past 20 years or more.

Where I came from, big hair is a status symbol; the bigger, the better. If someone gets married, the mother must have the biggest hair out of all the women present at the wedding party. Big hair meant you got your shit together.

So my aunts were coming to Singapore. I guess they had voted against migrating to Timor Leste. Not sure about my uncles.

My aunties always make an annual pilgrimage to Singapore, but this time, they were fleeing COVID-19. Or so they thought. This was just before Singapore realised that unless we shut our borders there would be a mass exodus from neighbouring countries looking for better medical care here. The old dames made it before the cut-off, along with one of my younger, unmarried male cousins. I gathered he was brought along to manage the luggage. Well, we Asians know filial piety: the woman carried you for nine months and expelled you into the world with great pains; if she said you come and carry the luggage, you better come and carry her luggage.

Getting down to business right away, I googled: "Best hairdresser SPACE big hair SPACE old ladies SPACE Singapore."

No satisfactory result. I tried all sorts of combinations of the sentence, alternating the word 'old' for 'senior', 'big' for 'beehive', added the word 'backcomb' and still I was no better off. I told Mum this just wasn't a good time. And why couldn't she recommend hers. She said the lady who did her hair was on a sabbatical, afraid of Coronavirus. There was no lockdown yet, but we all could feel it was coming.

I gave a shoutout to several online chat groups I was in to see if anyone's mum could recommend a traditional hairdresser at such a time. This is why one must have friends.

I love all my aunts to bits. Other than this hair business, they were the most cheerful and loving of people. They all doted on me. However, sisters were still going to be sisters at any age, be they 7 or 70. The four sisters bickered over day-to-day things such air conditioning, speed of walking and even angle of photography.

Upon my greeting them at their hotel they remarked how blond I had become and that my hair was a little too flat. I should add more volume to attract more men. Another aunt suggested that I should go for a religious retreat, so I might find enlightenment and following that enlightenment, perhaps a much improved new husband. I thought wryly to myself, yes, because hanging out with people who lived a vow of celibacy would be the best way to acquire new men. My aunts can be quite imaginative.

I thanked them and was not the slightest bit perturbed as I had developed the great skill of selective hearing when in the presence of elders. A skill I'm sure some of you have developed too especially if one was still single and unmarried during Lunar New Year.

They all expressed themselves most articulately from behind their masks. My aunts were no covidiots. And who says masks were a hindrance from talking, it clearly did not stop them.

When they arrived, their hair were all erect and defied gravity. Few days later, towards the end of the week, was the real trial. I received some leads from friends after searching high and low, that this and that hair salon would have the necessary tools to recreate such a hairstyle. You knew the salons would have one of those bonnet hood dryers, to set the hair. Once it's backcombed and set with hairspray, even a typhoon could not move the hair. That was the idea. It should survive a good portion of the week and even when they sleep; the next day it should look more or less the same. A little less puffy, perhaps, but respectably erect. In any case my second aunt preferred to err on the safe side and slept Superman-style, i.e. face-down. All in the name of beauty.

The hair salons normally were cheaply priced, hence the ladies preferred to wash and blow their hair there frequently. A cause and effect relationship.

My mum stayed home because the car could only fit five people: me, my three aunts and cousin. But lo and behold, the traitor had jumped ship. He was busy with his own errands and left me to deal with the grand dames and their hair.

We found ourselves in an older shopping mall in Orchard. There were two possible hair salons there. Let's call them Salon A and Salon B. Aunt Mei inspected them, was not convinced with Salon B's tools and chose Salon A. Salon A could take two customers and Salon B could only take one. They negotiated and sorted themselves out.

It was a good 1.5 hours of brisk walking all over the old shopping mall, waiting until they were all done. Before I left them at the salons I could hear my aunties describing in straightforward English, with animated hands going up and down, which no one can mistake that they meant 'big', and 'backcombed'.

The three of them emerged from the hair salons on opposite sides of the mall at about the same time. One had bigger hair than the others.

"Eh? How come your hair is bigger than mine?"

"Aiyah, I should have gone to your salon instead. This one the curls are too tight. Look like our mum's."

Though beauty standards have evolved over the years, women remain stuck to that era in which they looked their very best.

Seen from the car rear-view mirror were my three imports in the backseat, faces all covered with surgical masks.

Off we drove into the sunset, three 'helmets' blocking most of the car's rear windscreen, visible to any one driving behind us.

A tremendous success.

Anna

This chapter is written in honour of our departed loved ones, especially those who left us too soon during this pandemic, and in memory of my grandmother. May time heal all wounds.

In the face of the present adversity, we have a choice: to cry, or to smile. I have chosen the latter.

***

Anna. They called her 'the cheerful one'. Her death anniversary was coming but I wasn't going to be able to attend the memorial service this year, thanks to the bloody Coronavirus travel restrictions.

Flights to Indonesia had been suspended. Right now even funeral wakes are limited to just a few visitors at any one time. And if I were to return to Singapore afterwards, I'd be quarantined.

I was grateful I did not have to attend a funeral at this time.

Just before the lockdown, I shared the following story with Allen, my dear friend and neighbour, over dinner. I started to tear in the midst of it and he, anxiously tried his best to cheer me up, quipped that a mutual friend had erectile disfunction.

Quite peeved, I told him, "Allen, I really don't want to hear about anyone having ED right now, let alone that so and so."

Allen was more horrified with the idea of him having to comfort a crying woman in public rather than the thought of an unknown, dead old woman. Old dames (who were still kicking and alive) had started giving him dirty looks, all across the Italian restaurant, whispering to one another, "Oh, he cheated on her. What a snake. So bad. Oh poor girl. Didn't we know one or two in our time."

Little beads of perspiration started to appear on his temples, as he explained a little too loudly in no particular direction. "It wasn't me, it wasn't me! Her grandmother died, three years ago!" he volunteered.

They didn't believe him. I thought I'd turn this up a dial. Between the sniffles I sneaked in a wicked, "Oh how could you," and dabbed my eyes with serviettes.

My Oscar-worthy performance earned Allen more dirty looks as he phoned our other friends who were supposed to be there with us too, in a panic. "Where on earth are you guys? Get here, like, right now."

"It's gonna be ok. She's dead. She cannot feel anything anymore! Let's pray eh, tomorrow we burn paper offerings for her? What was her favourite food?" Allen continued in his appalling yet valiant effort in consoling me, upon calling for reinforcements.

This proposition plus the ED saga startled me for a moment and bought him just enough time before our friends joined us.

* * *

Several years ago, I arrived at the columbarium. It was a year after her demise.

Before the car even stopped, my eyes were already brimming with tears. I could not see very clearly and I'm pretty sure my eye make-up was running. I hoped at least the eyebrows had remained intact. It didn't matter, these folks could not voice their opinions anyway. I decided to follow Hollywood protocol and donned my big sunglasses. This trick made everyone look better immediately.

I ran to her niche, or so I thought. I wailed at that area for a good five minutes or so, wallowing in self pity, and reported to my grandmother how crap my life had been ever since she left us.

She was six years short of being a centenarian when she kicked the bucket, but still it did not lessen any wound for me. She was most precious to me and I fancied that I was her favourite.

My mind wandered to the past. For as long as I could remember everyone has had to put up with me because she, the matriarch, had said so. The truth was, I was a nightmare of a little imp but to her I was a faultless little cherub. My perfectionist grandfather could only grumble in silence even after I used his pristine bed as a trampoline. His bed would look like a war zone after my visits, which was every Saturday night, when my parents dropped me off at their place before date night.

Hence, the lifetime bond of the old woman and the little imp.

Suddenly something snapped me out of my reverie. My focus abruptly shot back to the glass box containing an urn in front of me.

Oh God. It was not my grandmother's. I had been smearing tears and snot on somebody else's box. I noticed a columbarium officer standing patiently behind me. He must have been impressed that the guy had been dead 20 years and his descendant was still so affected.

Apparently grief did not help my already challenged sense of direction and neither did the tears and the shades. I had to stop crying for a moment to check my bearings.

One and two. I took two embarrassing steps to the right, to the correct coordinates. Oh for crying out loud. They must have moved her again.

Her children could not agree on her final resting place. In their attempt to uphold democracy, deeming everyone who came out of her had equal rights regardless of order of birth, they gave all the columbaria a try.

In a true traveller's fashion, they had her moved around maybe six times, by car. My Gentle Aunt, always the one carrying that urn on her lap, sat in the middle of the backseat, flanked by her sisters.

One columbarium was too noisy. Another was too far. One had been deemed too expensive, and the alternative too close to the Protestants. The family were staunch Catholics and you know how fabulously the two groups got on since the time of Henry VIII.

Finally they decided on this location which was the original choice, a few kilometres on the outskirts of the city. And even then they had her shifted from one niche to another, until everyone was finally satisfied. Maybe it was her spirit as my grandmother had loved travelling and did not stop until she was 90. Apparently not even in death had she stopped travelling. This time, as was the tradition whilst they were alive, my grandfather had no say but to tag along with her. Her children had put their ashes together to love and bicker in one urn for eternity.

When I heard of my grandmother's posthumous travel story, I was so worried that the car might be 'kissed' inadvertently from behind by another car, given Jakarta's traffic. Then her ashes would be on the floor of the car, along with all the dirt. My brother, trying his best to console me, came up with a typically masculine solution.

"*Jie*, don't worry, I'll buy a brand-new vacuum cleaner. In case something happened on the road, we can vacuum Ah Kong and Ah Ma from the floor. It will be clean."

I bawled even more.

Back at the columbarium, the officer had placed a chair in front of the correct location. Now it may be the correct axis but not quite the correct height, at least not for me.

Grandfather was a six-footer whilst grandmother stood no taller than his shoulders. Even so, there was no question who was the tiger of the family, and I guess height differences were no issue for horizontal pursuits. They had nine children. It followed that the grandsons were as tall as him, and the girls petite, and guess who was the smallest one of all. Indeed I had taken after my grandmother. But what I lack vertically, I made up for by being the loudest.

Fortune had smiled upon us on that account. Imagine if it were the reverse, it would have been a weird family picture at the funeral parlour with all of us standing in a row.

I discovered that her niche was two spaces above my head. I muttered more complaints, thinking they must have chosen a cheaper lot, proportional to the male line of sight.

For readers' reference: in the real estate market for the dead, the most expensive plot is the one directly at eye level. For an average Asian, that is around 160cm from the ground.

Apparently the chair was given to me not to pray, but to stand on. I swallowed my pride and climbed on it. And shortly after, as if on cue, resumed bawling at the correct niche.

It was a simple clay urn. If I had my way I would have chosen a much more luxurious urn and adorned it with jewels, as she was very dear to me. But my wise mother had explained that whilst she lived, grandmother was a very humble person who led a simple life. The non-pretentious urn fit her very well. In the end, it was later replaced by a sturdier stone urn.

Throughout this story I have been referring to the urn as hers, although in actual fact it was my grandfather's too. He had died 22 years before her, from a simple slip in the bathroom. The Indonesian government informed us that the town planned to build a shopping mall at the location of his tomb. We were given the chance to collect his remains. So they exhumed him, wrapped his long bones in silk, and placed him on top of her body, where her heart was, the very last night before her send-off. Be careful who you marry, your kids will put you two together whether you want to or not. I smiled wryly. The old lovers were together again.

Superstition had plagued her departure. Catholics they may be, but some relatives were still influenced by Javanese belief and yet others by the Chinese belief of bad luck. Somebody had suggested that to ward off evil influences, family members bathed themselves in water with seven different kinds of flowers.

My mum's three sisters had discussed among themselves and the two older ones concurred that there was nothing wrong in following suit. They did not dare tell my mother as they knew she would scoff it off as superstition. So they procured a big bucket containing seven kinds of flowers and the bucket took a turn between their households. They were neighbours and lived nearby my grandmother too. For the grand finale, one of my cousins showered his car with what was left of the magical flowered water.

My youngest aunt had looked after my grandmother until the end, and had refused to participate in the flower ceremony as she did not believe that her mother who was such a blessing to others when she lived, could be bad luck in death.

My mother had gotten wind of it. The next day the four sisters were all seated in a row at the funeral parlour. Looking straight ahead, my mother took a jibe at her elder sisters, softly remarking, "*Jie*, you both smell good today. You smell like flowers."

"Ah, I only took a little bit. It was her (pointing to my eldest aunt) who took the whole bucket," said my flustered Gentle Auntie.

All of them broke out in laughter. The virtue of my elders: not easily offended and their ability of finding a speck of humour even in the face of grief.

That day of her cremation I insisted that I was going to be the one to accompany grandmother in the hearse. She always made an effort to send me off to the airport every time I left for studies overseas and whenever I travelled abroad in my younger days, I reckoned it was fitting that I should send her off for her last ride.

My marriage had been nearing its demise by that stage, but my Ex was present. He flew in late from Australia after being yelled at. He had skittishly suggested that he would follow suit in our family car behind the hearse. But with a glare I shoved him inside the vehicle carrying my grandparents' remains, next to the driver. I said that it would be most ungentlemanly to let me ride alone in that vehicle, especially as she was fond of him. So it was me, him and the driver. That seating arrangement unfortunately for him, meant that he was situated directly at the 12 o'clock direction and closest to the coffin.

My Ex believed in ghosts. I noticed he was scared out of his wits and was reciting *Our Father* and *Hail Mary* non-stop all the way to the crematorium, which was out of town. I kept turning to look behind at her coffin, reassured her and patted it once in a while soothingly. Every time I did this my Ex would freeze in horror halfway in his incantations, and had to start reciting from the beginning again as he had forgotten the sequence.

After all the ceremonies were settled, we went home. At the very last moment before the coffin was shut forever, I snatched my grandmother's well-worn shawl that was placed at the very top of all the clothes accompanying her in the coffin. Shortly before her passing, grandmother had also bequeathed her best sarong to me. I slept with these two items underneath my pillow for a long time after. My Ex and I had not shared a room for years then, but suffice to say the dead lady's sarong and shawl were most effective in deterring a man from sharing one's bed, thankfully ever again.

During the month when she was in the ICU and was about to kick the bucket, her grandsons took turns keeping a vigil in the hospital. A family representative was required to be present; to make a quick decision and to inform the rest of the family in case it was necessary.

The waiting room in that hospital was not made for anyone to stay over with old, over-stuffed chairs bound together, just like those old bus stations. How could one sleep seated upright? The room was also filled with other patient's family members keeping vigil.

The first volunteer was my younger male cousin who was just a year older than my brother. He could not sleep the whole night and fell sick the day after.

Next volunteer, my brother. He chuckled and declared that he would come fully equipped, unlike our cousin. He brought a rolled-up mattress, a pillow, a flask, his clothes, eyeshades and a big duffel bag containing God knows what.

Still, this warrior too could not sleep and for the rest of the week he ended up consuming a traditional herbal concoction, three times a day. Known as *Tolak Angin*. It was the remedy that Indonesians swear by to ward off any feeling of being unwell.

And then, the eldest grandson who was a true blue night owl, like me. He survived.

There is a running joke amongst our family members that great grandmother had taught her only daughter and then her granddaughters, that to have good luck and a good husband, they must work very hard and not sleep before midnight. This is why the ladies in our family are all night owls.

This questionable centuries-old obsession with getting a good husband who fit a certain checklist was perhaps exactly the reason why my family and I were phenomenally missing the mark in that department. But not to worry, onwards and upwards.

Now. Where are all those single dudes in the supermarket...

THE
BIRTH
OF A
COVIDOL

A Covidol is Born

Once I was a Covidiot, a true blue Covidiot. YOLO was my motto, whereas social was my middle name.

March is when my birthday festival takes place every year with lively celebrations occupying every weekend that month. I threw parties, the bigger, the better.

My convenient excuses were: too many friends, the function room could only hold so many, and to avoid public altercation of friends who did not get along with one another.

With approximately 140 invitees, I also faced dilemmas as such: so-and-so were not speaking to so-and-so; so-and-so used to sleep with so-and-so (and was now sleeping with another so-and-so, and hence must not mix with so-and-so and their current beau); so-

and-so was a business competitor of so-and-so; and so-and-so just hated everyone.

It was a headache to organise all these events but I did it nevertheless as I loved them all.

I am a hugger. I hugged everyone at the party. Those pecks on the cheeks the Europeans perfected? I made it mandatory. Right-left-right, right-left-right-left if you wanted. A touch of good ol' Europe in Singapore's heartland would not hurt. On your face, not the south cheeks.

This year though, there was a slight modification. Guests were promptly greeted with sanitisers and ushered to the washbasin, whether they wanted to or not.

I planned to use an infrared forehead thermometer but my purchase did not arrive on time and to stick a thermometer into each guest's ear would be preposterous. So I dispensed with temperature taking. I was brave. I was a Covidiot.

This was the time when Covidiots, such as I, thought we were untouchable. It would happen to everybody else but us. Or so we thought.

"Don't be paranoid," OR

"It's everywhere lah, if you get it, you get it. All of us will die one day anyway," OR

"Singapore's medical system is so good, we will be ok."

These were our most common delusional slogans, our brave warriors' cry. We were touted as the best in the world with how we dealt with the Coronavirus pandemic (until Taiwan overtook our laurels and we became Miss Runner-Up. Now, Hong Kong and New Zealand are ahead of us, and we are not even Miss Runner-Up).

Stay home, they said. You'll be safe, they said. I stayed home. The virus came to my home one fine Sunday afternoon. My neighbour was an imported case. "Love thy neighbour," at this moment not.

I heard the news from another neighbour. The 'import' arrived on a Thursday and was warded on Sunday.

This shook me up quite a bit. The children were staying with their grandparents over the weekend and I told them to remain there for their safety. Especially after the grim news that same day that Singapore finally recorded our first two COVID-19 deaths.

There was speculation as to the nationality and gender of this unwanted 'import'. I said definitely must be European. Blame had shifted from the pangolin-eating nation, as Singapore had shut its borders to all of Asia, Italy and Iran at that stage. The obvious choice.

My dad said he or she must be Indonesian (prejudices according to our own set of experiences), but I said cannot be because the Singapore border had already been shut a week ago.

My neighbours' speculations ranged from Chinese to Indian. Some days it was a she, some days she became a man, basically nothing was off-limits.

When you were once a Covidiot yourself, you were even more afraid of other Covidiots when we changed allegiance because we knew EXACTLY how Covidiots think. How they moved, where they hid their gatherings… masked as 'Staying at Home' i.e. staying for a few hours at other people's homes.

Having turned to the other side (imagine a vampire bit you and you were now one of them) I proudly declared myself a newborn Covidol.

A Covidol was someone who observed all the government's protocol and advisory in combating COVID-19 in the country, the polar opposite of a Covidiot.

Upon my catharsis I hunted other Covidiots, with judgements ablaze, from home.

My apartment window had a lovely view of a popular jogging track beside the Singapore River. It was in actual fact a very large ditch by any other definition but I preferred to think of it as a river rather than a glorified sewer. It's all about perception, people.

"Ah! Look at that foreigner not wearing a mask! They think they are Superman? See, running so close some-more," were my unsolicited commentaries to my long-suffering domestic helper, who was also on a 14-day, self-imposed house arrest with me and the hamsters.

* * *

Hello?

Are you wearing a mask?

Where's your sanitiser?

Stay Home!

Repeat after me:
"I.... (insert own name here) will. not. be. a. Covidiot."

Soprano in Quarantine, ACT 1

"What's the strangest thing you've seen in April, out of your window?"

Yes it's all coming back to me now. So, the neighbour got COVID. The rest of the neighbours and I weren't served a Stay Home Notice (SHN) but being a responsible, newborn Covidol, I stayed at home and isolated myself. Alone.

DAY 1

I turned on the radio. Belting out of it was *All By Myself*, my new anthem. Hmmm. Switched to another channel. Here comes Tiffany's *I think we're alone now*, another anthem.

Yes, yes, don't I know it.

This must be a message from the Universe. This is my payback for being a partying Covidiot all this while.

First it was the insects. Now this depressing playlist.

Earlier on I hurt my back while saluting the sun (a yoga pose). It was not sexy. Could it be the twists or the downward dog? A friend recently said all this indoor doggy business didn't seem to do me much good. Sitting on ice, not Disney on Ice was the aftermath.

Seeing as I would be on a self-imposed solitary confinement for 14 days, I made a list on how I should amuse myself and keep myself occupied. But for now, let's order food.

DAY 2

Start the day by watching a friend's most ardent recommendation, *Spartacus*. It's basically men in skirts with women not wearing skirts (or anything at all), like the epic movie *300* minus the budget and Gerard Butler. Hmmm. Maybe I'll continue later, or not.

Late afternoon. Time to phone a friend, six of them, located in Singapore and across different time zones. It's cheaper than talking to a shrink. Calls are free anyway. After all what are friends for.

What next? Grab Food!

DAY 3

Lovely morning. Ah! My old faithful opera scores! Nope. They're all postponed for the year. Oh well.

I suddenly recalled my friend Jonathan got me a pair of binoculars for my birthday. I had suggested (not very subtly) when asked, that I wanted a new pair of opera glasses. Instead what he got me were this pair of massive, green bird-watching binoculars. He said it'd do the same trick. It was so heavy that if you threw it to a swan in a pond, the animal would sink. I expressed gratitude but I wouldn't be caught dead brandishing it in a concert hall.

"Hey, this is good stuff man! C'mon, who wants some hoity-toity useless opera glasses so small you can see better without it. Birds or humans, this will enlarge everything! Function, babe! function over looks."

"Jon, like seriously, who does birdwatching in a condo?"

"Well, I'll be checking out some birds by the pool with that thing if I live in a condo," came his flippant remark.

Anyway. I thought it might be a brilliant idea to check on neighbours. Just to make sure they're OK. No, not spying, BIRD-WATCHING.

I looked through the windows and swept through the balconies to try out the binoculars' features, adjusting them as I went. Surprisingly, it was quite good. Peaceful. In case you don't know, I wear glasses when the situation merits, and have to take them off when using the binoculars. Then the objects would be magnified, by virtue of the binoculars, and fattened, by virtue of my astigmatism.

Neighbour no. 1, hanging clothes on the balcony. Not supposed to.

Neighbour no. 2, breakfast on the terrace. Very stylish. This was more like it.

Neighbour no. 3, watching TV indoors. Errr, no, something was bobbing on the sofa. They were…

Oh, by the pool! Kids' teachers having some quality time in the jaccuzzi. Poor things. They don't have any privacy here do they? I should tell the kids and their classmates to stop snooping on them on the condo grounds.

OMG! Just saw another neighbour with binoculars too! You see me, I see you! How cute was that. And it's a bloke of acceptable age!

[I waved]

He saw, and shut his curtains. What the….? Hmmpff! His loss.

Time to eat. Back to basics, *Indomie Soto* with egg and cut chilli padi tonight. Yum.

DAY 4

The air-con must have blasted in the night. It did not work. Fantastic. I had to sleep with my windows open. I was even scared to call an air-con technician in case he had Covid too.

8.30AM. Got woken up by the shrill sound of a recorder. It looked deceptively harmless but was far from it. It was an instrument of torture. I thought I heard the last of them in secondary school.

Oh, for goodness sake. Who in their right mind would practise the recorder at this time? Not everyone had a piano or a snooty string instrument, but a recorder, everyone could afford. Just go to Daiso (the nations' favourite budget store where everything is priced at $2).

This recorder ordeal carried on for the rest of the week, as my windows had to remain open.

First puff, "*Preeeeettttt…!!!!*" Loud and proud (and flat). Must have been the mother showing by example, or testing if the bloody thing worked.

Second onslaught, "*Preeet. Preeet. Preeeeettttt….*" It was supposed to be a Do-Re-Mi but with less air than the earlier one. The poor kid carried on for the whole one octave.

See, this was the thing about recorders in school, it's basically a one-octave instrument. Upon reaching the higher 'Do', none of us knew how to reach the notes in the next octave. Well, I never figured it out. Thank God my current instrument doesn't have 11 holes.

Third onslaught, even more jarring. Must have been the mother again, or the nanny this time.

Oh, God. Please make them stop. [Covering head with pillow].

Ahhhh, cannot sleep. Let's order McD's Big Breakfast.

DAY 5

Solo Zumba! The wonder of technology!

More Netflix.

[Finger hovering above the Food Panda app].

DAY 6

Spent the afternoon reading Felix Cheong's *Singapore Siu Dai* in the bath, with jazz music in the background, and a glass of *Pomerol*. Saw it performed at the Arts House recently. It was hilarious, definitely beats watching men in skirts killing each other. Lovely, lovely. Life can always be worse.

I wondered if the chicken rice shop next door was open and which app did delivery for them.

DAY 7

Hadn't been sleeping well the past couple of nights without air-con.

A friend who's really into everything natural, recommended a sleeping machine which played sounds of the Amazon rainforest. She said it did wonders for her. In the absence of such a machine I beamed the file onto my bluetooth speaker.

It was disturbing though. Along with the calming crickets symphony, the frogs were given some random, trumpet-like solo parts. Woke up me up a couple of times so I reckon I would make do without the frogs and the forest.

Today I will try that new blueberry muffin mix I bought last week. Success! Well it is basically the muffin version of instant noodles, but still, I made muffins.

Spent the rest of the day watching lectures on this wonderful app 'Master Class'. Ah. Invest in one's growth! Loved Bobbi Brown's make-up lectures.

Buzzer ringing. Al Afrose's *Nasi Goreng Kampong* had arrived.

[END OF ACT 1].

A COVID Fairytale

11

Once upon a time, on a tiny tropical island, there lived a Princess.

An evil witch had cast a spell upon the common folk and people were dying. The curse ravaged the kingdom's inhabitants.

The King of the Red Dot Kingdom swiftly decreed that no common folk should step outside the castle moat, on pains of a $300 fine, if they were caught the first time around, and then $1,000 if caught the second time around, and if they were very, very naughty, they might be put away in the palace dungeons, and whipped. All in the Kingdom were henceforth ordered to wear face coverings! They faced the same punishments should one be discovered without. The palace historians called this face covering, a mask.

The King decided to lock up his only daughter in the highest tower. No one was to step in, and she could never step outside. She only had her lady-in-waiting, and her pet hamsters for company. And Netflix of course.

Sadly for her, her hair may be somewhat long, but alas it was not as long as Rapunzel's and therefore not long enough for anyone to climb up. Beautifully coloured though, because as soon as the King made the decree, the Princess fled to the palace hairdresser to have a last-minute tincture on her hair.

The same punishment was to be applied to any man attempting to break into her tower, be he noble, or common. She was guarded by a mini dragon that circled the tower day and night, with phone camera and penalty tickets at the ready, to report and punish anyone who might be out of his mind.

Condemned to live alone in the tower, the Princess was very sad. She spent her days looking out of her tower window, and wondered about life, and her many, many suitors.

But the King (and the Witch) had underestimated the bravado of overexcited young hormones. Several Princes from faraway lands had heard about her plight.

As an exception to the King's decree, anyone who managed to evade the mini dragon's sight, and somehow entered the tower, could stay. However, he had to stay with the Princess in the tower and could never step out for the duration of the Evil Witch's reign of terror.

But this could only happen, if the Princess allowed it, by removing her surgical, blue face veil to show her consent.

Days passed and the suitors circled the castle moat, devising strategies on how to see the Princess.

The first Prince arrived on an expensive white horse called Beemer. He came bearing a few bottles of magical grape juice from faraway lands. To brighten her days, he said. The Princess' lady-in-waiting accepted the gifts gracefully, and the Princess observed from afar, but her veil stayed on. The Prince and his horse took their leave.

Another suitor came on foot! This time bearing fish; Japanese (the fish, not the Prince). He laid his offerings outside her door, with a lovely note, that should she see fit, it would be lovely to see her without her veil, if just from the window. Her lady-in-waiting reported from the tower's secret peeping glass that it was so. But still, she would not show her face.

Dire times required desperate measures. A Prince came disguised, wearing the green livery of a Grab palace messenger. They were the only ones allowed to move about freely in the Kingdom at this time.

Another gift, by her door. And when the Princess opened her tower door, he was there, in his green Grab livery, but he was no messenger. Distressed, the Princess slammed the door on his face, but not before taking the gifts by the door. Sadly, he too did not get to admire her lovely countenance.

The next Prince came on a red horse, took her by surprise, and begged her to stick her head outside the tower window. He proclaimed loudly loving entreaties, in the style of Ethan Hawke in *Great Expectations*, underneath her windows. Well as I always say, love makes everyone stupid. It was all very romantic until the neighbouring towers told him to shut up. What party poopers. So he too, had to depart without seeing her full face, never stepping into the tower.

The same Prince sent a message via a digital pigeon called WhatsApp, of his brilliant, lazy idea. He would move into her tower and change his address. Her brief reply, "Declined."

But love is ever resourceful. An exotic suitor observed all of these attempts. He summed up that their offerings had not been good enough. He would send her a very special fruit, with spikes, not easy to procure in the Kingdom at this time. He was sure that it would make an impression. He had sent his very own pet frog to deliver it. Indeed it made an impression but at the wrong tower. The Queen, the Princess' Mother, was a huge fan of durians, thought it was a lovely surprise and devoured it right away by her regal, queenly self.

The Princess soon got wind of this unfortunate news, sighed, and signed up for Tinder.

Soprano in Quarantine, ACT 2

The second week of isolation.

DAY 8

Bird in room situation. Stretching out with my eyes half opened.
Aaaaa! There was a black bird (no, not the bad omen one) with
some yellow stripe near its beak hopping around on my make-up
table. It must have come in through the open windows.

Shoooo. Shoooo. I hope it didn't carry Coronavirus. It went out,
finally. Where were the Dettol wipes...

Got up and contemplated if I should do as the Italian opera singers
do and sing at the balcony. Or out of the windows in my case. One
just had to adapt.

It would be the popular choice, *O mio babbino caro.* That would do. As I took a big breath, filling up my lungs professionally, about to sing out of my living room windows…. There was fogging.

I had forgotten it was Thursday and every Thursday they fogged the whole complex.

These were the subtleties of living in the tropics. On top of Coronavirus we had these little killers, dengue mosquitoes. But by God, I loved living in the tropics. There's no need to wear a lot of clothes.

I frantically closed all windows, lest all kinds of insects came flying in. Well, my five minutes of fame just had to wait.

What else should I do…

DAY 9

Following the ominous fogging, even more so than usual, I noticed a new trend of insects in the flat; more varieties, in greater numbers. This week, I counted at least four types of creepy crawlies that had ventured into my abode. Previously, it was almost none.

I conjectured once with friends over FaceWine (group Facetime) that perhaps this is the universe's way to reset. Humans had done too much harm to nature, and now with lesser humans going about outside, nature had taken back control. Definitely more insects.

Creepy crawlies and I never get along. There was one occasion my friend Jack and I encountered a baby tarantula at a friend's place (they treat it like a pet), and we ran out hand-in-hand together. Oh, correction, it was Jack running away first. I followed suit.

But now, this human needed to eat. Have recently joined this Restaurant Rescue group on Facebook, I would order direct from the vendors. Let's support them.

DAY 10

Continuing my Sir David Attenborough moment. Then there was the bane of my existence, the roach. I can never understand why some creatures were part of the Mighty One's creation. Why must a cockroach, or say, a crocodile, be one?

In the evening, book in hand, hot roasted Japanese green tea at the ready. Very civilised. It's that time of the night when one is enjoying her solitude and thought one is completely alone... but for a six-legged companion.

Hey, I've met snakes and reptiles, but in my experience they were all two-legged while this breed tonight is not.

Yes, it's all coming back to me now.

Now that sound. That alarming sound. The scary sound of its layers of wings, like a bunch of crepe papers crushing. I'd recognise it anywhere, a bane from my childhood.

In my earlier years, sometime in the night an insect fell down and disappeared into the side of my single bed. I ran all the way into my brother's room.

"(Sleepy) *Jie*, what on earth…??"

"Cockroach, in my room."

"Oh."

My brother understood fully the horror and went back to sleep. Two of us in a single bed. Mind you, back then he wasn't a six-footer. I was still bigger than him. So the bed fit.

DAY 11

The weekend is here! Actually it's a Thursday, but everyday is now a weekend.

Time for a virtual, online group catch-up session with my ladies!

This was all the rage these days, catching up online with friends for sanity's sake. Thank God for technology. We could at least see friends that way.

Somebody set it up on Zoom, and one by one we joined. At that stage it was discovered that Zoom had some security issues. A hacker had sickeningly showed a picture of male genitals to primary school students, but it was the least of our worries and if we were to be flashed with such a scene, we won't be in distress. Nothing we hadn't seen before.

Topics discussed ranged from updates re personal life, family life, work, exercise and then the wretched Home Based Learning (HBL).

Personal Life. No, nothing juicy, zero updates on who was sleeping with who, because we all knew we were all bloody staying at home. So unless you're married or had a steady partner, it's a very solo sleep until further notice.

Family Life. This Circuit Breaker really made us evaluate our relationships with the people we lived with. In the best scenario, we got to know our family members better. At worst, we heard of people who were suffering from domestic abuse and were stuck at home with their abusers. Really hope they receive some help. Some of us exchanged stories on distressing sounds we heard from the neighbourhoods and vowed we would report to the authorities if we found out anything untoward.

Work. This was challenging! Lines and times had been blurred. So long as you were contactable, you were at work. Oh Lord. Everybody concurred we should shut our work devices off after 8pm.

Exercise. Varied feedback. In our group was a health influencer who could do five classes of yoga and pilates in a day and not be dead. Oh, did I say that she's done the Iron Man Challenge too and was able to drag a truck tyre? She is not representative of the general population. On the other spectrum was Miss 114 Steps a day, from bedroom to kitchen. Yes high on the topic were the trackers we used to track how many steps we took at home. And the apps used to keep fit indoors.

HBL. Those with kids know this best. Don't even get us started. Doomed, we are doomed. This was war. Attack of the cling-ons! Why, oh why? Hanging by a thread, we were.

What a nice opportunity for a pyjama party, and to reconnect with our loved ones.

DAY 12

Called the kids and folks. This was done everyday but so as not to be repetitive, I just highlight it once.

Kids were happy and well. Chat with the folks revolved once again on the challenges of grocery shopping. Online delivery lots were full, they told me anxiously. What were the tactics to obtain delivery slots, short of sending their only son to the 'jungle'.

DAY 13

"Hold the item in your hands. If it does not spark joy, thank it for its service in your life, and put it in the discard pile."

It's KonMari time! Moi as well as many of you have utilised this period not just to binge watch TV shows, or learn a new skill, but also, to spring clean. And what other methods were better than the one invented by Mari Kondo.

Found many, many things, from jeans I'd be delusional to say I would ever fit into again, to a curious descaler. I forgot why it was found in the bra drawer. There were just a lot of things. We all hoarded. And what a refreshing feeling it was to offload.

DAY 14

Finally! Finally!

What was a lady to do when this was her last day of self-inflicted house arrest, knowing her babies were on the way to her anytime now?

Rest and binge watch. Self-care.

See you all on the other side.

[END OF ACT 2].

The Music Room

What did we lose in April?

"Cancelled!" Everything was cancelled! Concerts, cancelled. Operas, cancelled. Even the puppet shows were cancelled.

There were some events I wish could have been cancelled over the past decade but it certainly were not these.

Coronavirus. The word reminds me of an airplane advertisement that promised, "We'll take you to places you've never been," upon its fleet going under the sea twice in the same year. I've never been to that place. I'm pretty sure those hundreds of people had also never been (and did not wish to have been). That unfortunate advertisement was soon withdrawn, for obvious reasons.

April landed us in strange terrain.

We all had to go through the unfamiliar experience of being cooped up at home with family members and partners 24/7 for months. There is such a thing as too much of a good thing, even if we do get along. Little did we know that we were required to be at home for that long. Our rapid week-by-week transition of emotional roller coaster ranged from trepidation to optimism, to the monumental grievances on depleting dishwashing liquid and the lack of grocery delivery windows. One would spend an hour ordering supplies online, only to discover during checkout that delivery windows remained elusive. Rinse and repeat. Everyday was Groundhog Day.

On top of these daily challenges, we were all suddenly thrust into the limelight and had to become movie stars and tech experts. I'm talking about teachers, lecturers, artists, students, office workers, and most people who had a job.

However, humans are resilient. How fortunate we are to be living in the digital age! Not to be outwitted by the Coronavirus, lectures, lessons, and almost all meetings, could now be shifted online. Except for some minor glitches with regards to this so-called technology that these meetings heavily ride on.

Take for example my fellow musicians and I. We had to swiftly shift to the streaming method in delivering our three main activities of rehearsing, performing and teaching.

Some parties manoeuvred more successfully than others in adapting to these new circumstances. What I found surprising, for instance, was that children took to online music lessons like ducks to water.

"Yup. I was more like a DJ. Since students muted their mics and turned off their cam, I sometimes felt like I was talking into the void. I was like a DJ on-air," another lecturer friend who taught a big group further attested.

In actual fact, teaching and learning music online consumed twice the energy of doing so in person. It was after all a vocational thing. One had to be shown how to do it physically and physically replicate it after. Opera singers for example, are vocal athletes. During these online music teaching and learning, we all had to make a strenuous effort to decipher two-dimensional non-verbal cues, with every silence possibly interpreted as a dreaded tech glitch.

The string of endless "What?" or "Sorry, I couldn't hear you," repetitions, imbued by missing syllables (or notes, in my case) became our new normal. We figured that out soon enough, but we made do.

On the field of live music presentation, we are after all performers —musicians, singers, dancers, actors. Put us in front of a camera and we will perform.

Rehearsing should be just about the same, or so we thought. How difficult could it be?

Until we discovered that our fates depended entirely on the internet.

As I discovered through my own experiment on rehearsing with a pianist via Zoom, it was akin to being stuck in a dial-up time machine when the rest of the world had gone 4G. When the internet was out of whack, I was out of sync.

In the spirit of adapting, the rehearsals pressed on, but let me tell you of one such saga.

Recently I had to rehearse a piece from Pergolesi's *Stabat Mater* for an online recording that we were planning to air during this lockdown period. It was to share the joy of music with the public. I had performed that well-known sacred vocal work previously as the soprano soloist at Singapore's first national theatre and concert venue, the Victoria Concert Hall.

Just to elaborate a bit on the work in layman's terms: it is a baroque piece from the 1700s, a church vocal composition depicting the Stations of the Cross. Its lyrics (written in old church Latin, not Latin as in Latin American) describes the suffering and the steps Jesus Christ took towards His crucifixion at the Cross. In a music store, shelved under the category of Sacred Songs, or arias, as we call them. They are not operas but an earlier form, perhaps opera's predecessor. There were several composers writing their own compositions with the same title.

The piece I happened to be doing out of the 12 solos and duets in the work was titled *Fac ut ardeat cor meum*, a beautiful duet of soprano and alto. I'll get on the pronunciation in a moment but the piece was basically a fast chasing, repeated steeplechase of the song title, one after the other, for pretty much the entire song.

The tricky bit was the pronunciation of the lyrics itself (and its unfortunate meaning in modern language) and that the internet kept freezing.

Let's break it down into manageable parts. Latin after all is an archaic language these days that only highly-ranked Princes of the Catholic Church understand. Emeritus Pope Benedict, by his own admission, said that if he had bad news to tell the Archbishops that would potentially ruffle their feathers during his daily sermons, he would deliver it in Latin, because only very few would understand enough Latin to complain.

My solo parts involved me singing, "Fac Ut," predominantly.

'Fac' sounds like 'dark' without the 'r'. Does it remind you of a certain four-letter word? Yes, that is it. You can probably very easily guess how this word is pronounced. It is indeed that highly-versatile (yet misunderstood) four-letter word we are forbidden to say in front of children.

'Ut' on the other hand is pronounced 'Oot', not an Australian 'ute'.

The internet was not at its best that day and its glitches meant the 'oot' parts were skipped quite a few times, and all we could hear were the 'fac' bits.

It became an aria about 'fxxx's, repeated 50 million times in under three minutes by two women singing high and low. Hey, three minutes is a long time. A lot of things can be achieved in three minutes. Just ask Indonesians and their population of hundreds of millions.

How ironic for the lyric's venerable meaning. This is what happens when we sing songs written by dead people.

After the first two technical glitches, and many missing 'oot's in the making, in his attempt to help us, the frustrated pianist sweetly remarked, "FAC. Loud and proud, you two," referring to the strong, crisp pronunciation of the consonant 'K' at the end of 'fac' each time that word came up. He thought enunciating a muscular 'fac' might help with the internet problem.

Now that about ruined the piece for me. It took all my being not to laugh whilst singing it. For the next two minutes I could not do it. I could not sing it with a straight face. It was distressing.

Channel anger, my Director had instructed, a tip to keep a straight face in such circumstances, when we were practicing for the performance some years back. Channel the feelings of stress and woe. Oh how easy it was to channel those feelings these days.

That was also the same things she helpfully suggested when we both went to a benefit concert in support of a mutual colleague who was performing. At one part of that performance, the prop and singing were so mismatched, involving a mummified, gaping, neon cockatoo resting on the outstretched arm of a garrulously dressed male opera singer, who was struggling to reach his supposed high notes in the piece. It was a mini-scene where the hero in the story (i.e. him) had to descend to the abyss to find his dead lover. It was not meant to be a comic piece at all but the combined effect of the incongruous prop and singing were hysterical. We struggled to keep a straight face but I did not manage as well as my esteemed senior.

Of all people I understand fully a performer's pressure to perform in front of a paying audience. It was a tough job and I highly supported the efforts every performer made to bring about a performance. But on this occasion I could no longer hold the fort.

I pretended to cough and employed other ingenious self-distracting methods so as not to laugh during the show, mindful that we were seated right at the very front row facing the performers and there was no escape. At some point I deliberately dropped the whole content of my handbag and pretended to crawl underneath to collect the items scattered on the floor, to the disapproval of other concert goers, just so I could hide my face.

Towards the end of the stuffed cockatoo's aria, I finally pulled open the programme and decided to plaster my face with it, pretending to read. I thought that would be discreet. I only realised later that I had covered my face with the programme upside down.

* * *

The Arts, and theatres all over the world, are in a crisis mode as we speak. Many are wondering just how few of us will be left to continue our craft when the pandemic was over. We make a living not just by performing but also teaching to ensure a regular income. Both fronts are in dire straits. One music teacher friend has sadly conveyed that he was losing students. During this online teaching period, many parents have opted out, as they too are facing their own challenges, and find online music learning too draining.

My Simple Sally explanation is that some paid online initiatives better commence very quickly. Facebook, for one, is trying to let artists charge for online performances, so that we can somehow monetise our crafts, or governments really must come to the rescue. Otherwise the world will end up with one hell of a monochrome society, when the Arts, considered a non-essential, is dispensed with altogether.

On a grassroots level, let us all do our little part to support artists. Lest we wake-up one day and find that they have all become lawyers. When all you have left on TV is the weather forecast, how blue will thy life be then, oh, little one?

And I Pronounce You, Man and Wife

Once upon a time, man had lived happily, on his own, in the Garden of Paradise. Man was contented, being naked all day long, not having to work, not having to report his movements to anyone. He was getting along just fine on his own with the animals. Then God, his Almighty Creator, thought how lovely it would be, if man were not alone. He was given a friend, a companion to enrich his life so to speak. God created a prototype, followed by an industrial factory system, so He didn't have to do things from scratch each time.

"You know what? I'll make one more of this hoo-man, so these two could then multiply themselves and I'd just sit and watch. I don't have to keep fashioning clay. I'd better things to do, like, create more comets, or whatever." I'm guessing that was roughly what God was thinking, just more eloquently put. God took one of man's ribs and made it into her.

And then there were two. Man woke up one day and discovered next to him there was a creature who looked just like him, only much prettier and it came with soft round features. For a while they were both naked (although they did not realise it), not working, no children (meant they didn't have to do bloody Home Based Learning) and were having a really good time.

Little that man know that not only he was missing one rib but that this companion was going to give him an accursed, forbidden fruit. He let her convince him (what a Lady Macbeth), and that was the beginning of the end for humankind. See how well that turned out: man was doomed to hard labour his whole life and she was accursed to forever bear children in great pain. The children remained another kind of pain for the rest of her natural life.

During this lockdown, part of my questions on our existential crisis was that, had we as man and woman worked out how to live with one another just yet? Ever since that rather monumental mistake of eating that fruit.

I hypothesised, after thousands of years of living side by side, that we had not.

The battle over toilet seats, up or down, and the invasion of 500 beauty products into a man's bathroom space upon his fairer better half moving in, were common conundrums for those who had experienced a co-living situation. No wonder that men then created 'The Man Cave'. They all just wanted to go back to the way things were.

And while spending more time with your significant other might sound ideal to some, many couples were realising that the things they typically found endearing about their spouses were less enjoyable when they became a permanent fixture in their 'workplace', too.

During this Community Circuit Breaker (as it has been named in our region), or lockdown as globally understood, couples have had to live in the same vicinity 24/7.

Now, I might love you and you might love me, but do we do so, 24 hours 7 days a week? This plus the angry, dreaded terror called PMS, every month, for every female of child-bearing age. It did not seem to make things too optimistic for men and women to be together under one roof, without venturing much outside.

Let's see how this panned out for quarantined couples. I had to do some market research as I was single at the time of writing this piece. Sorry to disappoint but there wasn't a man lying around in my abode at the moment. I just checked.

Time to phone a friend, a video call with my best friend *du jour*, Jenny. I asked her my million-dollar, simple question,

"Hello! How was it like, living with a man, during lockdown?"

I had to shout the sentence over several times, as she had a husband and two boys. It was somehow very noisy on her side. To answer my question she angled her phone camera towards them. All three of them were jumping up and down doing pillow fights in her living room.

Shortly after that conversation, I gave a shoutout to friends on social media, if this lockdown had been a 'loveboat' or a 'potential double homicide' in the making.

Some couples were loved up, meaning, they didn't work together (or didn't need to do much work from home at all), plus had no kids on lockdown with them. Best scenario ever.

But my research focused on those couples with more interesting predicaments. After all, it ain't news if it was not bad news. So I approached some couple research in a scientific manner.

Exhibit 1: Female, early 50s. In general happily married. No kids.

"My husband is driving me up the wall. Men have no idea how to stay at home, do they? He and his beer cans, he and his socks. All day, all night and this perpetual tapping sound."

Exhibit 2: Male, early 40s. No Kids. Allegedly separated but as neither he and his estranged wife had another home they had to be locked-down together, just the two of them. Two bedrooms and a flat of misery. They had been moving in an orbit around each other all month. There was no running away.

He: "(whispering) I'm avoiding my wife."

Me: "(whispering back, needlessly so, in the spirit of camaraderie) Oh you poor thing. Where are you?"

He: "In the toilet. Oh, Blistering Barnacles, there she is again, shouting for me." And then dial tone.

Exhibit 3: A happy Italian couple with four kids and way too many monitor lizards coming into their backyard, scaring their young bubs.

After the fifth monitor lizard came into their backyard this month, the wife solemnly approached the husband while he was happily having his afternoon coffee (a self declared barista, a new hobby he had developed during this period). She asked in her usual matter of fact manner, "Amoré, which one of your golf clubs you no longer liked? You know, the one you no longer used?"

He indicated a club and resumed his coffee while watching his basketball game, while she got up briskly, took that golf club and went to the backyard.

Unbeknownst to him, she had set a trap for the monitor lizards attached to their kids' trampoline. Using food bait she had a very effective rope trap. I had no idea how on earth she achieved this but let's just say I don't want to piss her off, ever.

She had to choose between her crawling babies and lizards, and the choice was obvious. One had tried to attack her youngest. The pest control never came on time, if they came at all. Time to take matters into her own hands. Oh, did I tell you that she was a Major in the army, and that her expertise was manhandling men? Lizards were included, apparently. Well the two creatures might sometimes share some common traits, if you asked me.

True enough, one greedy monitor lizard was dangling on one leg from the trampoline rope set-up.

She was indeed an efficient woman. She put the lizard into endless sleep with a few effective, powerful swings. It was done as quickly as she could, for a swift end. The deed was completed in under a minute. Then she called the pest control, for disposal.

The husband had finally thought it curious that the wife was going to play golf at that time of day, in their backyard. He had gone to check on her, and watched as the scene unfolded with his mouth open, hands by the sides of his face, screeching, "My club, my club! Oh, Dio!!"

Well they were after all Italians. A passionate breed, you know.

The wife reported there were less lizards venturing in. As for the husband, he was interestingly very nice to her after that episode, as one would guess. There were no arguments between them, with him replying very agreeably, "Sí, Amore," on all her requests for help around the house. And he plied her with much, much wine. I wonder why.

Ahem. Moving along in our scientific discussion,

Exhibit 4: Tiffany, one of my best friends, happily married. No Kids. Not intending to.

In the midst of our lively video call nearing midnight, her husband popped his head onto the screen, to say hi. She glared (but lovingly so), and told me that he wanted food again, for the umpteenth time.

I wanted to ask, considering the time of night, if it was really a full meal or another kind of dessert that he wanted. Hey, we ought to be happy for those who do not have to resort to self-entertainment. Not everyone has to be as miserable as us.

Exhibit 5: A young couple with a young baby. A happy couple by all appearances.

Here is some background about them. She was breastfeeding full-time. He was on conference calls from home. He was also very bad with multitasking full-time.

As she was hanging the laundry to dry on their balcony, he happened to be on a conference call, and had absentmindedly locked his wife out on the balcony and walked away while talking with the office. She knocked, yelled, did jumping jacks behind his back, shouted some more (this time with expletives) but he was none the wiser. Only when the baby cried for more boobs did he look for her and realised he had locked his wife out on the balcony. Suffice to say she had a lot of feelings to convey afterwards.

And then there were also those who worked together, at home and at work. Oh my, the can of worms.

Exhibits 6: My favourite same-sex couple. Australians. No kids, or not just yet. Thinking of adopting (I told them they were out of their minds).

They were an architect and an interior designer who worked together and had agreed to keep things professional at home. The architect called me to say that his better half had been searching for inspiration in the bath along with a dozen scented candles for a good half of the day, alleging he needed to de-stress, when a Skype call came in to his laptop, and I overheard his partner saying that the music was too loud and he was welcomed to join in the bath, after he finished work.

Sweet.

Finally.

Exhibit 7: Man in his early 60s, latest wife half his age. Kids (his, of course) no longer at home.

My friend, a high-flying investment banker, had married an aerobic instructor (yes that breed was not extinct). Lucky wife no. 3.

"Hey, hey. How's lockdown? Short circuited yet??"

In the meantime, highly audible from the adjoining room, "One, and a two, and a three, and a four! AND ONE! And a two, and a three, and a four!"

I guess to each his (or her) own.

Let us observe further how these all panned out when there were one, and a two, and a three, and then four people in the next chapter.

"Go Forth and Multiply..."

In the beginning, there was only Cindy. Cindy had been lucky in love. Cindy met Olivier, the love of her life, at a house party. He was French (didn't we all have a Frenchman fantasy at some point or another), whilst Cindy was an international lady of Indian descent. Brahmin, of course, the posh ones.

Cindy and Olivier had a son. Let's call him Alex, a handsome mixture of East and West. Olivier, for their 33 years of marriage, divided his time between Europe and Singapore; Europe for work, Singapore for family. Their grown son Alex, had also come home recently upon completing his sports science degree in Australia.

Two plus one equals three.

When the lockdown was announced, agreement was reached amongst Cindy's siblings that her home would be the best place for their mother to stay for the duration. Cindy's mother had the habit of staying at her children's homes in turn.

And then there were four.

Cindy's elderly mother arrived with her very own lady-in-waiting. So then there were technically five.

She was originally hired as a helper and companion to Cindy's elderly mother, but had much difficulty in fulfilling that post so she ended up just focussing on cleaning the home. And waited. Hence the moniker lady-in-waiting.

All five were cooped up in Cindy's 130 square metre, three-bedroom apartment. It was a small flat according to Cindy. The small flat was actually a mini-penthouse with sprawling views overlooking central Singapore and Marina Bay Sands. Could always be worse, I told my friend, over drinks at her place a lifetime ago. It could always be a glorified sewer adorned with non-law abiding Covidiots like the view from my window.

Cindy's (or at this point, *their*) place was literally a melting pot of cultures with *nasi goreng* (Malay fried rice) as their proud national dish at home. Later on it was chicken rice, as we were about to find out.

This is her account on surviving lockdown with her family.

"Until February this year, the household was not over-stretched. There was my mum, and her aide. At that time the aide had just arrived and I had many visions of my mom being kept company and engaged by someone else other than me.

Anyway, that was not working out and we were now waiting for the flights to operate so the aide might return home. The crux of the conflict was that my mum and her aide speak different Indian dialects.

Note to readers: there are Indians, and Indians. The same goes for Chinese, and Chinese. As I have discovered, just because people look the same it does not mean we can communicate with one another. For example the Hokkien dialect is entirely different from Cantonese, and in the absence of a unifying national language, well, imagine Bill Murray and the Japanese, in the movie, *Lost in Translation*. Communication breakdown.

Then in February, my 23-year old son sauntered back from Perth in Australia after having completed his university education. I did not know if this was a blessing. Now he had no excuse but to get a job. Get a job, mummy said! That's how it started with me and him. The story of my motherhood.

Then my shining expectations diminished in this order :

- Apply for 20 jobs per day
- Secure an interview
- Update your CV
- Do a relevant course online

- Go and run outdoors
- Get out of bed before 10 am
- Now, just get out of bed before lunch

Oh yes, no excuse but to get a job I said? Well, obviously there was a valid excuse! Bloody COVID-19.

Next, the husband.

The thing about Olivier, my very own Frenchman, he usually lived where he worked i.e. Europe. He had slowed down work in everywhere else in the world of late, upon receiving his permanent residency in Singapore. He moved here, bit by bit, as in lots of bits.

All this happened within two months! Coincidentally, the uninvited guest by the sexy name of COVID-19, decided to visit planet earth just about the same time too.

I always looked forward to Olivier's visits. I would take his clothes out of the boxes they lived in, let them see daylight, and hang them up in my already bursting-at-the-seams closet. The day I forgot to do this, he went out to IKEA and got his own closet and miraculously found a large enough spot in my, I mean, *our* bedroom.

His plane would land at ungodly hours, which meant that I had to get up even earlier to get him at the airport. Then I got the brilliant idea of booking him a limousine service and I was relieved of that wee hours duty and I considered this money very well spent. Oh, and I even got him his own keys to my, I mean, *our* apartment.

He had left Singapore for Moscow in early March this year and returned before the Stay Home Notice (SHN) came into force for visitors from Russia. And therein began our living together!

I just realised that in the entire household, everybody had a room for him/herself except for yours truly.

In the beginning, I had to stay as far away as possible from him. Although there was no SHN for him, he had just taken a flight. So 14 days gone.

Then on April 4, I had the brilliant idea of going to Mustafa Centre at 5 am to get groceries and toiletries. That night, Mustafa (a well-know bargain department store situated in Little India) closed its doors for the ruthless COVID-19 had decided to visit it. And our number of cases increased to an unprecedented level ever since.

I washed and disinfected everything upon hearing the news that I was amongst the last patrons at that store. So as my husband's 14-day self-imposed quarantine ended, mine began.

To make matters worse, I was one of the 20 tour guides handling the ill-fated Italian cruise ship that was denied embarkation in all of Southeast Asia. Singapore allowed them to land, the passengers were transferred by bus to the airport, and they all went back to where they came from. Although some not immediately so, they were stranded at the airport hotel, I heard. This, plus that Mustafa episode were tales that would be repeated at our dinner parties in future, when we could all gather again.

Thankfully, the two of us emerged unscathed. We started working out together—decipher working out as you like. But my version was that we would run up Fort Canning Hill every evening. We liked running late to avoid as many people as possible.

Fort Canning Hill was, once-upon-a-time known as the Forbidden Hill. It was said that spirits of the other world roamed the area and so the common folk would stay away. Obviously Olivier and I did not consider ourselves common folk. Alas, Minister Lawrence Wong announced last week that everything had to be done solo so we were no longer able to run together.

My home, oopps, *our* home had absolutely no outdoor space so I was very happy when beloved Olivier, my 'new' housemate, would go down to the pool and camp there for the next few hours with his unlimited-4G internet. That was short-lived as one by one, our facilities, places that were supposed to facilitate life, were shut down by government order.

Yesterday, Olivier got thrown out from the 1 x 1 metre space that he paced around every afternoon next to the pool. Sigh, this meant he would stay in my, oops, *our* room!"

Cindy told me that the first couple of weeks were madness at home. It was like a labyrinth of languages. On a typical day, one step out of her room, Cindy would bump into son and husband arguing animatedly in French, then husband turned to address her, in English. She took two steps towards the kitchen and discovered mother and her aide had been arguing in both Bengali and Hindi (each sticking to their own language and both equally confused), with Cindy then mediating in sign language, for mother and aide.

I told Cindy her family must have all taken a sip from that magic cup that Prime Minister Lee was seen drinking from, to transition from one language to another so smoothly.

"War-of-words in each and every permutations continued daily. You name it, we had it."

Her son even stormed out one day without his mask and had to cower back with his tail between his legs when he spotted a police officer patrolling outside and realised his folly. The bliss when one wins! Haha!

Cindy continued: "It was very hard in mid-March for a couple of weeks. We all had to get used to each other's idiosyncrasies and moods. Not happy, go to your room. I didn't have my own room for I was always the bigger person and let Olivier have *our* room.

How did we spend our days?

For over 14 days, I did not visit any shops. I was in a self-imposed quarantine. Olivier would go to NTUC Fairprice at Killiney Road at 1am. And there would still be a queue at the cashier.

My husband and I had always had different sleep timings. I'm a lark and he's an owl. I would doze off at 9.30pm only to be woken up by him at midnight because he had just read something online and needed a listening ear on the latest COVID-19 development. Once up, I could not sleep until three hours later. Yet in the morning, I woke up before anyone else, fixed healthy beverages and breakfast, then lunch, then rest, followed by study, run and finally dinner. I don't think I've ever juggled this much, not even when Alex was little. Because you see, Olivier would often be travelling. Alex had his own schedule, I had my own social and fund-raising life. And of course I did not have an elderly parent and a helper at home.

These days I enjoyed a little lie-in and I woke up late. In my dictionary, that was 7.30am. I drink a concoction of grated white and yellow ginger, crushed black pepper, juice of half-a-lemon, a dash of honey every morning as did my husband.

Note to readers: see? The Indians know what to do. We should just follow suit.

"He hated it but now had gotten used to it. That was pretty much my breakfast together with coconut pudding.

Then I started to plan the menu for lunch. Today was a herb and cheese encrusted baked salmon with a gratin dauphinois. If that sounded heavy, it's because it was! Evening meals were always a salad and if we were feeling adventurous, a *nasi goreng*.

We all gathered in the living room for the helper to clean the rooms and bathrooms. I was thankful for this time as it would be impossible to get father and son out of their rooms if I were the one to clean. We would discuss the incompetence of the world, the degradation of humanity, the triumph of the animal kingdom who come out to watch us being locked up, or down.

When all was clean, they retired back to where they came from and I took my place at my newly-placed desk to reflect on the world via Facebook. Words of wisdom and cute kitty videos kept me company until I went to cook. For an hour or two, we were all in our own space, in our own world, in *our* small flat.

Lunch was usually home-cooked but I struggled to make it interesting and novel. Most of the time it was unnoticed—according to them, just a run of the mill menu that took me two hours to prepare! And they didn't even add the time, cost and potential risk I took to get the ingredients!

So order-in lah! Just that from where? I wanted Pariaman's *nasi padang* but apart from *nasi goreng*, Olivier saw nothing was interesting. But *nasi goreng* was my go-to dish! Why pay good money for it plus delivery charges for something where the ingredients were sitting in my kitchen?

So for the next few weeks, the apartment inhabitants had a change of national dish to Olivier's favourite chicken rice until even he said he was beginning to grow feathers.

So then how? Cook lah. First go online and pick your ingredients and at the end of 30 mins, you will be told, no delivery slots available. Sigh."

Wasn't this the story of our lives, that elusive delivery slot, I mused.

Cindy sent a message the other day, that everybody else had the comfort of their own rooms, at hers. Of late she had gotten very good at sitting at her desk and shutting the whole world out. A desk which she lugged closer to *her* living room windows, and now overlooked the Marina Bay Sands and the Singapore Eye (as opposed to a wall, or sewer).

I guess we can all adapt.

The Mask Crusaders and
The Second Wave of Covidiots

Towards the tail end of the lockdown in Singapore, I witnessed something astonishing first-hand. It was the proliferation of the second wave of Covidiots.

In anticipation of measures being relaxed, people had started to congregate in large groups, like along the river at Robertson Walk. Dozens of them at a time.

On my way out to the grocery store the other day, I encountered this grandpa without a mask. He was not running, he was just strolling along the jogging path, admiring the river. Not two metres away from the grandpa, directly on his 3 o'clock direction, most shockingly was my daughter's former teacher and his young family, out and about in the neighbourhood. Iron Man, Miss Potts and their infant daughter were heading to the grocery store without safety masks on. I guess a family who can fly around in iron suits could afford to.

Along the way, people who didn't look like they ever exercised have now become marathon runners, dragging their highly visible excess kilos with them.

Then there were the groups of Filipina domestic helpers, gathering in droves. Pushing prams together, not distancing at all, masks barely covering their noses.

Seems like a $300-$1,000 fine was no longer meaningful enough to discourage such behaviour. To me that amount was terrifying. On the other hand I was starting to wonder if these people with too much money at their disposal could be my friend. I promise I'd be a very good friend. I was open to receiving donations: food, wine, gold bars, just not somebody else's husband please.

I wondered what it would take for people to take things seriously? As we speak, the country where I was born and everywhere else, people were dropping flat on their faces daily like nobody's business—at the train station, on the road, at the bank. Yes, they must have all died of flu or tinea. No, not AIDS. No one's had that much fun these days.

I noticed that the Germans, always on the forefront of technology, had pioneered the use of swimming noodles secured on top of people's heads, as in hats. An ingenious social distancing measure, made mandatory for their café patrons.

"This be you and me soon," I mass-messaged friends wryly.

Alright, world. We gotta up the ante. Soon we would be released back into the wilderness, out of lockdown. The world needs to come up with a Covidiot spray. Something that would turn people into frogs or turn their facial colour purple (or worse, turn them into their mother-in-law), if they were not social distancing or a non-mask wearing Covidiot. Short of throwing a bag full of cobras at a group of congregating Covidiots, I'd say a Covidiot spray might be our best bet.

On this note, forces on the Covidol opposition bandwagon have taken matters into their own hands. Taking the higher ground of civic duty at the cost of possibly having tomatoes thrown at them, they had taken it upon themselves to be the mask crusaders.

A mask crusader had graciously reminded a fellow bus-rider that his mask had fallen below his nose. Perks of public transportation. The Covidiot looked as if he was told he was not wearing any pants (though one could not help but compare the two parallels). If looks could shrink anyone, my friend would be an ant by now, so much for public spiritedness.

Another mask crusader walked past a man sitting on a bench without a mask, with his laptop on, without a care in the world. He was accompanied by a bottle of beer. The mask crusader reminded the lounging Covidiot that he should be wearing a mask, and that he should be at home. Ignored, the mask crusader decided to flash his phone camera (a global weapon of popularity destruction), to take a photo of the Covidiot.

Alas, a mere 1% battery power left remaining. He could but just take one photo before the phone died. Covidiot with the laptop was none the wiser though, and hastily put his mask on before scurrying home.

I guess it is true: with battery comes great responsibility.

A Nation of Tarzans

The announcement came too late, at a cheeky 9.30pm, that all basic hairdressing services including men's barbers were to be suspended when the clock struck midnight. This suspension would last until the end of the second round of Circuit Breaker, six weeks later. The suspension included other non-essential places such as bubble tea shops, dessert shops and pet shops.

This breaking news came two weeks into the Circuit Breaker. The 5pm address to the nation was by Prime Minister Lee Hsien Loong.

He spoke well as always, and again that magical cup that allowed him to change languages with ease every time he took a sip, was there. It was a message delivered with a smile. That further tightening of the Circuit Breaker was deemed necessary, understandably due to the alarming rise of COVID-19 cases in recent weeks.

My WhatsApp messages exploded first with agonised parents with no hope of salvation, since the torture of HBL (Home Based Learning) was to be extended a further four weeks, making it another six more weeks. We had just gone two weeks into it and barely survived.

Next, were group chats woes on bubble tea, and finally, it was the dire hairdressing issue. Men thought they had the last laugh when auxiliary hairdressing services such as perming and colouring were banned. They had all expected us women to emerge with bi-coloured hair at the beginning of May, which was the original end date of the first round of the Circuit Breaker. One had given me a call over the weekend, just for a laugh, at my expense (well, what we wouldn't give, for a laugh these days). Little did he know that in a few days' time, he would be in the same Bad Hair Day boat.

"HAHAHA! Eh, I'll call you, ok! I'll call you in three weeks' time! See how your hair looks like then! (He peered into the video camera) I see you went for a colour just before the Circuit Breaker, looks ok now. Ha, I also went for a haircut same time as you. Immediately I called my Japanese hairdresser at Scotts, he said I was the first one who called for appointment. Then the whole city came down to his shop."

My fancy friend worked in the judiciary system. Well even when one's day job was sending people to the dungeons, one might prefer looking good doing it.

Now who's got the last laugh. I sent him a simple text that said, "Video call, 31st of May. Will check on your ponytail."

At the thought of all of them looking like Tarzans come 1st of June, immediately that very evening photos and reports of men flocking to barbershops and hairdressers all over the nation filled the internet and social media.

Very long lines. As if it was free collectible Hello Kitty time at McDonald's again. The Government was not to be outwitted this time. Last time there was lenience, we were given four days until the Circuit Breaker, which caused jams and queues at every mall (obviously I was amongst the throngs of Covidiots) to shop for every last minute perceived necessity, such as kids' Nintendo games (for sanity's sake, these were absolutely essential).

No such leniency this time. The Government Multi-Ministry Taskforce meant business. Announcement at 9.30pm that such stores were to be closed one minute before midnight at 11.59pm.

I sent out a mass message to my male friends (inherently to poke fun, knowing it was too late) that they were to make appointments with their hairdressers ASAP, before they had to resign to the inevitable. In any case there was already a marked trend of gentlemen sporting a 5 o'clock shadow, or by now, beards many days over.

I concurred that if one were to look remotely like say the unrealistically good-looking Jason Momoa (think *Khal Drogo* and *Aquaman*), one was never in need of a haircut. But unless you were 6 foot 4 with more pecs than I could count maybe a haircut would prove beneficial.

Trust me, I counted very carefully at close range to the TV screen. I put it on pause. And don't forget that face, even when he didn't speak he was still so pretty.

Before my smug mass messages could reach them however, most of them were already panicking anyway. Group messages, and no less than nine individual messages came at a cross. Few men had worried about bubble tea.

"WTF?"

"Going to my hairdresser now. I think I still can make it."

"Wah. Why PM never say earlier? It's 9.30pm leh! I asked about McDonald's on Facebook also he never answered."

"[Swearing in Hokkien], [swearing in Cantonese], [swearing in English]."

I suspect that last friend must have had a sip of water out of a magic cup as well, to be able to express himself clearly at will, in three dialects too. He would have done the PM proud.

I offered some practical solutions to my male friends' woes. I said they had some options.

• Aaron Kwok's hair in the 90s. Literally, and I mean literally all my classmates in high school were sporting this floppy hairstyle whether it suited them or not.

- Mullet hair. When would be a better time to sport a mullet hair than when only your mother could see you?
- Man Bun. David Beckham pulled it off. But he was after all, David Beckham.
- Jason Momoa. With faith, you could look like him, especially after a few pints of beers for both you and me.
- Japanese Yakuza.
- Samurai Hairstyle.
- An Afro.
- Or just go Bruce Willis and shave it all.

Someone actually listened to my suggestion and immediately bought a shaver online, express delivery.

My dad had a gleeful phone discussion that night and remarked what an asset my mum was, seeing that she had been the one cutting his hair for a long time. Lucky man. He was indeed a very clever man who knew to hang on to a good lady as he had one. My old man won't emerge from the Circuit Breaker looking like Tarzan. Watch and learn, gentlemen.

My brother had followed suit. He reckoned getting his hair cut by mum would be his best bet. Not that he had any choice at this stage.

This was a necessary measure. I guess not to be upstaged by the decisive, female New Zealand Prime Minister Jacinda Ardern, ours decided it was his turn to announce his decisive measure as well.

Quoting from a recent hilarious account of Italian Mayors reacting to people inviting mobile hairdressers into their homes as their citizens were not abiding by the measures to stay home and distance: "Mobile hairdressers? I don't understand why you all invited mobile hairdressers into your homes! Do you understand, it will be a closed casket! No one, will see you. It will be closed. There was no point, to have your hair perfectly styled! Who would see your well-coiffed hair when you are in the box? No one!"

They do explain very well, don't they?

[Texting my hairdresser furiously to get an early appointment for 2 June].

Coronahair

18

Twenty-twenty. The year of bad hair and things not going according to plan.

"Mum, what's wrong with his hair?" my kid whispered to me upon being presented with the view of her teacher looking slightly unusual during their Google Meet class check in. My daughter was wondering why after two minutes he suddenly went into audio mode, citing bad internet connection on his side. I struggled to keep a straight face. It was the hair. He had Coronahair. It looked as if an over-eager mini lawnmower went over the middle, eating up at least 2/3 of his hair and was not quite finished with the rest (how's that for a lesson on fractions, ha ha ha).

He must have been one of those gentlemen attempting to shave his own hair, and upon realising that the razor worked faster than his hand and not to his advantage, he must have turned it off. Just in time for the Google meeting.

Hence my earlier view that a man bun would have proved a superior option to mowing one's own lawn. The only way his hair could have been fixed was to shave it all off, a safe option which more of his kind had resorted to, or to have left it alone in the first place.

How ironic it was that in the 1970s, Singapore banned long hair for men as it was perceived as a sign of decadence. Thanks to this pandemic, long hair for men might be making a comeback.

Little did we know that this year was to be the Bad Hair Year for all concerned. With the hairdressers completely shut upon for the extension of the lockdown, in an attempt not to look like Tarzans, people had been trying to cut their own hair, with hilarious and often regrettable results that may outlast the quarantine. It's safe to say most people's hair won't be looking its best at this time. For men, women and queers alike.

More testimonies from the survivors of Coronahair.

"I look like Sigourney Weaver in *Alien 3*," one male friend complained. He had self-administered a haircut with a shaver sans mirror. How very brave of him. I commended his valour. I encouraged him to audition for the movie *Alien 4*, maybe as an alien instead of Sigourney Weaver, as he was clearly the wrong gender. But then again this was the age of equal opportunities, for both aliens and heroines alike.

Another had his mother perform the haircut. It looked like his mother had placed a bowl upside down on his head and used an electric razor, resulting in the back of his head looking like a palm tree, with a coconut-top effect and strange, close cropped hair at the bottom. A failed attempt at the currently popular men's fade cut. He sent me a photo of that unfortunate attempt: a lopsided bowl cut.

On the other side of the island, someone could stand his unruly wavy hair no more. He enlisted his wife to trim his hair. He now sported a mullet.

Some decided to follow the celebrities and shave all their hair off, a la penultimate Hollywood action heroes Bruce Willis, Jason Statham or Vin Diesel. However this look apparently did not quite work for everyone. It only worked if your head was highly symmetrical. Egg heads, long heads, bumpy heads don't really yield a Hollywood result.

When others with God-given symmetry on their heads do not possess the adequate tools to execute a close shave, they end up with prisoner hair with bumps on their heads.

This conundrum sparked a slate of interesting self-haircut video tutorials. Generic titles along the lines of "How to cut your own hair at home in 2020" garnered tens of thousands of viewers. From which camp, one could easily guess. For some reason, the men in the instructional YouTube videos were always in the bathroom, and always topless. I guess it was so that there was less cleaning afterwards.

Upon careful study of these videos, the men had their predicament ever so slightly improved: a passable hairstyle in the front, but with the back of the heads completely messed up.

Finally they figured they needed a new trend to complement the new look. A beard. According to a certain men's magazine, a beard instantly pushed up any man's attractiveness ratio. It made all ladies hot and heavy (going by that article, Taliban men might be the gold standard).

A lot of men were seen sporting this new trend of 5 o'clock shadow. While the hot and heavy had yet to be proven, to the relief of all wives and girlfriends, professional hairdressers were thankfully allowed back at work to save the universe.

ON PARENTING & HOME BASED LEARNING (HBL)

A Strategic Alliance

Few people find queueing riveting, but we all have to do that. For a parent, there was nothing like the panic of being locked-up (or was it locked-down) with kids for a month or so in a flat without ammunition.

Here's what I wished had happened, other than for the pandemic to never have existed. It was for me to live happily ever after with an unreal Prince Charming in an air-conditioned chateau somewhere. And to never have to queue for hours to buy kids' entertainment items when there was possibly a super spreader or two in the crowd.

But alas, the lockdown. When our Prime Minister announced it, we were given four days to prepare ourselves. If you thought the preceding toilet paper debacle was bad, this one took it to another level.

Take my friend Linda. As a knee-jerk reaction to this news, she ran like the wind to the gaming shop and bought all the Nintendo Switch games that she could get her hands on, all $900 worth of them for her young son. I followed suit the next day, on a much humbler scale, picking up whatever was left that Linda hadn't bought. Lawyer-turned-banker Linda had always been proven right. Just ask her husband.

Single people were off to the hairdressers for a last-minute colour or perm, or waxing parlour for some 'gardening' in advance. Others desperately filled up their calendars with catch-up appointments with friends they had not seen for decades. Suddenly they could not wait another month. As for the young singles, the most royally irreverent of all the Covidiots were the ones who participated in farewell parties in clubs and bars before all the establishments were shut.

All of us modern parents were wondering, how were we to keep these kids occupied? Gone were the days where every Sunday I would alternate between counting the rock formations at my family home backyard and having a conversation with my dog. There was no TV for kids in the afternoon. I had no siblings then, just Don Vito Corleone for company, my pet German Shepherd, not its namesake the gangster godfather my Dad named him after.

First things first, attend to yourself and then to the child. That meant personal grooming. Everything that needed to be there should be there (like the highlights in my hair), and anything that needed to be removed should be removed (not going to elaborate).

Top of the off-to-prison shopping list were kid-related items.

My sentiment on food was no need to hoard, as we had discovered supermarkets would remain open, and going to one would be my best entertainment for the month. Soon enough I discovered that wine could also be home delivered, so there was no more cause for panic in that department. Anyway the supermarket nearby sold saké too (i.e. Japanese rice wine). My earlier over exuberant attempt to make one was a complete failure. I couldn't pummel the rice enough to make saké so I just had to buy.

I further observed that shopping before lockdown was a mission imbued with military-like strategies.

- You could go guerrilla over the four days to a lot of places either solo or in a team (for people who value future mental health over physical health).
- You could also opt for a tactic of divide and conquer (very popular with the Dutch) with friends or a spouse to different shopping points, with each of you getting loads of one category of items and then bartering it.
- Those on the slightly dogmatic side might employ some 'diplomacy' i.e. talking to yourself in an attempt to calm yourself down and directly head online to secure delivery slots rather than a confrontational strategy of braving the deadly crowd (possibly some of them carriers or already infected).
- There was also the option of exercising some kind of democracy at home, where you gathered everyone to discuss what needed to be bought, what were the desperate necessities (other than toilet paper) and if the kids could re-use whatever entertainment

tools they already had at home. People belonging to this category normally lived in big houses with a private garden and pool, and hence could afford to play hide and seek at length within their own abode.

Upon assessing the strategic options available to me, I concluded that democracy of any kind won't work for a two-bedroom flat dictator. Ain't no time to vote. Neither did I have a spouse.

There was no choice but to be absolutely revolutionary. I would just torpedo the whole island and run in all directions like a camel on laxatives with some fluidity in terms of strategy (as in I changed my mind by the hour as to which military strategy I'd employ).

I would also work with other similarly mad women with cohesive strategies in tandem. And in the night, when everyone was asleep, I'd go online, a combined adaptive approach.

After this nasty COVID-19 business, it had become apparent to most of us that more women should have been put in charge of world peace (how dare they call us emotional). More women should have been made generals. Women do get things done. The countries that survived best and earlier, were the ones with female leaders, such as New Zealand, Taiwan and Germany. Perhaps a better result could also have been achieved through feminine persuasion rather than the testosterone-laden decisions of World War 1 and 2 (and thanks to Trump, perhaps the impending WW3). See how well that turned out.

If the shops won't open, what would I need? As many world leaders had discovered, the most brilliant ideas were conceived while sitting on the toilet throne.

I decided to brave the crowd at Plaza Singapura, a centrally located shopping mall, taking along my domestic helper (a sub-general) for some queuing reinforcement. She could hold the fort in the queue while I flew all over the place, annexing more fiefdoms in the mall. Or at least that was the plan.

En route, I was told by our taxi-driver that the crowd in IKEA was impossible. It was not until I saw the images on the news that I knew how incredible it was. At least half of Singapore was there.

When one was willing to put one's life on the line, it was a holy cause. Perhaps one's sanity for the month was a cause worthy of such risk rather than drawing a rather obvious verdict deeming them all as Covidiots.

I thought it best to consult other 'multinational household generals' fighting their own battles elsewhere, to check on different battlegrounds status. People (especially women) were faster than any news network. First-hand info, or first-hand gossip, whichever came first.

My neighbour Heather was busy conquering several shopping malls in Orchard Road. She said don't head there, she'd get me what I needed from there. I returned the favour for the other items that she needed.

Upon disembarking at Plaza Singapura, the first order of business was art and craft supplies. By God the line snaking just to get into the shop was an hour long. But I must, so I lined up. My domestic helper had suddenly disappeared into a store nearby and couldn't seem to hear her phone so I was on my own. Another half-hour to pile items into the shopping basket along with other parents hoping to save their sanity, and another hour of lining up for the cashier when the said domestic helper finally materialised with her own shopping bags in tow.

Next pit stop was Toys R Us. Essential items: board games and Lego.

There was literally one box of the original Monopoly left on the shelves, my laser-vision told me so, while I was skimming through the various rip-off versions. I reckoned if my kids were to be playing Monopoly they might as well learn useful property buying skills and not collect rainbows and unicorns with the *Trolls* the movie version. A teenager and his dad headed over from the opposite direction, aiming for the box too. Gotta pull a Singaporean and be completely *kiasu* this time. I literally ran to the shelf and grabbed it. Shame took a backseat. I needed it more. Those two could converse the whole month instead.

Linda had given me the contact for her Nintendo shop supplier and that's where I headed to next. My girls had given my dad specific instructions as to what exactly to get and he read it to me over the speaker phone from home while I elbowed other parents with similar intent in the shop.

On the way to the taxi stand before bartering items with my fellow mums, I passed by a woman with a big hat and dark sunglasses, seemingly not wanting to be seen in public, with a shopping crate full of Rodial Boob Job tubes. I guess certain things needed to remain perky even if the apocalypse was looming ahead.

Funnily enough though, for me the real panic buying when the lockdown was extended the second time around was over pet food. My hamsters. Let me tell you why this was so.

For some others, it was that whole business of bubble tea. This was a historical moment with some literally filling up their fridges entirely with bubble tea, having conducted their very own Amazing Race to several outlets in the span of hours that same evening after the announcement.

My glorified rodents had gotten accustomed to be fed with factory-made hamster food. Someone suggested Marks and Spencer. No such luck there. Should I try feeding them carrots? What if they died? They'd be another Coco the Goldfish who was perpetually in the animal hospital. I was not ready to gamble on that.

Heather's kids once had a goldfish and one day it appeared to be semi floating in its bowl, not looking fabulous. When it finally performed a full float while the kids were at school, Heather hastily told them that Coco was sick and that Coco had gone to an animal hospital for treatment. They believed her, but then her kids were so much less suspicious than mine. On all good intent I went to a pet shop afterwards and purchased an orange goldfish thinking all goldfish looked alike, so Heather could tell her kids that Coco had recovered and had returned home. Eh, voila, problem solved. No? She freaked out when she saw my imposter Coco, saying, "Red! Red! Coco was red! Not orange!" Well, back to the pet store for me. My bad.

I couldn't possibly pull that animal hospital excuse off with the lockdown in place and besides hamsters could not exactly be flushed down the toilet. I would argue that there was substantiated cause for panic.

Epilogue

Post-War, some six hours later. Sinking on the floor of my apartment surrounded by bags, and more bags, as far as my eyes could see. I ought to get a medal.

I was furiously wiping each package with tons of disinfecting wipes like it had gone out of fashion. At the same time I manually counted if I had enough crayons, jewellery making beads, puzzles, Legos and board games to last a lifetime. One couldn't be too prepared.

Home Based Learning.
A Survivor Recounts Her Tale

It was Day 5 of Home Based Learning. I looked at my two kids through bloodshot eyes and wondered how quickly time passed us by. They were once cute and could not speak. In fact, there was once only one. It's a bit hard to fight if there was only one. Now there were two and they just would not stop talking.

Prime Minister Lee announced his plans for a Community Circuit Breaker a week ago. His way of delivering bad news was like breaking up the gentleman's way. Unlike the Pinoy's beloved Duterte who basically just wanted to shoot everyone.

PM Lee had explicitly avoided the technical word 'lockdown', so as not to inspire further mass hysteria. As if we needed more inspiration. For those looking down on us and saying we were merely a tiny red dot nation, for a start, please observe our impressive Prime Minister. He delivered his address in three languages. Every time he took a sip out of the cup at his side, he spoke a different language. Now people were starting to wonder what was in that drink. Which other country's PM could do that? So please stop complaining, lah.

We were also decidedly united. We were rational and in control of our own emotions, as could be seen by the 5km long snaking lines at the supermarkets today, with everyone pretty much having the same emotion. An increasingly predictable occurrence just before the PM's public addresses. PM about to give a speech, we go to the supermarket.

I had an emergency plan in place. I had it all figured out. The moment the Circuit Breaker was announced, the kids were going to have a strict schedule:

- Wake up at noon
- Sleep at 6pm.

For the hours in-between:

- Bath (1 hour)
- Meals (2 hours)
- P.E. (1 hour)
- Mindfulness meditation (1 hour)
- Me teaching them all 6 subjects (1 hour)

Next, I mentally assessed my prowess as the default Home Learning Teacher.

Art

Couldn't draw to save my life, but you could make do without the Arts, they said. The same people who were all watching moving pictures with audio soundtrack on TV now. Nothing to do with the Arts of course.

Music

Ah, could do. They would both be opera singers.

Languages

Doing well, doing well. I'd teach them a foreign language. I could teach them Indonesian with my eyes closed. Forget English and Chinese, too commonplace.

Science

I just plunged a Redoxon effervescent tablet into water and it fizzled. This should count. It was chemistry, wasn't it?

Physical Education

Would replace recordings of P.E. teacher with Chris Hemsworth's exercise routine when he was training for Thor, and run it on repeat. The kids would be more inspired.

Mathematics

Hmmmm. I knew for a fact that at least four of my kids' teachers lived in my neighbourhood, and if, by some pure coincidence, these learned individuals chanced upon my kids or my kids just happened to chance upon them (at their front door) with a crate of Heinekens (Would 6 suffice? No. I'll make it 12), wonder if they would be so inclined to teach Mathematics.

Maybe they missed teaching. Maybe they missed my kids.

FOUR! Four teachers! Ah! I chose well when I selected this neighbourhood to end up with such a teachers-infested cluster. I might not have a garden, but I had teachers as neighbours! Haha! Look who has the last laugh!

"...I look like Mummy... You don't look like mummy. You were adopted." One of them started crying.

This last sentence jolted me back to earth and I suddenly recalled what I was trying to do, seated across them. I was repeatedly drumming the tip of my index finger on their worksheet, with my dinosaur-like, unmanicured nail to restore order.

By the way this was how girls fought, with words. Ever since I ruled thunderously, "keep your hands to yourself" to make them stop pulling each other's hair, they have invented another way to make each other cry. I guess being trapped in a small apartment 24/7 was not bringing out the best in anybody of any age.

My friend Jenny called earlier for an emergency venting session, while hiding in the toilet. Her boys didn't use words, and instead settled their scores physically as little men would. It didn't help that her husband now worked from home too. Her toilet seats were all up. She lamented. We just didn't win either way.

In the midst of that illicit hushed conversation, one of her sons asked if she was inside the toilet and she yelled back, "I AM NOT

HERE!" She quickly informed me that she had been discovered and the line went dead.

It's time for some massive action, some serious teacher hunting before my kids found out how dumb their mother actually was. I thought I spotted one, from my toilet window, getting a tan by the pool. Maybe he would like a crate of beer.

But before executing this ill-conceived plan of mine, I put on *Frozen 2* on the TV, for the 50th time this week. I made a discreet exit right at the harrowing start of *Into the Unknown*. Disney probably already knew about this pandemic before it happened. Just look at the title.

A slight detour to the neighbourhood wine shop for some essential hoarding would not hurt. A few bouncy steps later. It was closed.

I was beside myself. How could it be closed? How could a wine shop be considered a non-essential? And haircuts were essential? It was especially in this day and age that wine (rather than a haircut) was absolutely paramount for a parent's mental health, seeing as we were to be home school teachers for God knew how long and at the same time, daydrinkers.

This generation was going to be The Homeschooled Generation, taught by clueless daydrinkers. God help us all.

If I had to choose between emerging out of this break, or whatever they called it, looking like a short-circuited, bi-colour haired

Tarzan or be without my grapes, I'd choose grapes any day. (FYI: the government suspended all hair perming and colouring services and allowed only haircuts at this point). My hair might not defy gravity, but I was at least less aware of it.

Well I reckon I'd check out the supermarket in the mall next door to see if there was any beers left. Human beings are known for their ability to adapt, you see. Some famous biologist (was it Dickens? No. He was a writer) said that the species which adapted would survive. I intended to survive. I went to look for beer. And if I didn't survive at least I had those two hair-pulling little trolls who would continue my legacy, whatever it was, I couldn't think of one right now.

I stood in front of the beer aisle. It was almost empty. Only one miserable, dubious sounding brand was left. Seemed everybody else had their priorities right during the panic buying.

No. I would not stoop so low.

Maybe I'd make my own saké from rice at home. Let me Google if I could do that. I reckoned if I pummelled that bloody rice to oblivion and fermented it, it would be more or less the same. How hard could it be?

I went home empty handed, with no beers or teachers.

I decided it was high time for some kind of play + exercise for the kids. I had a tremendously different idea about what play + exercise constituted for adults, but let's focus on kids for now.

"Let's play indoor golf."

"Yay!"

We designed a make-shift, indoor mini-golf course around the living room. My eldest swung her golf club, copying my awkward demonstration earlier. Her golf club went and hit me right in the shin. I sat down on the floor, grimacing in pain. From then on, my mood went further downhill. Like, how much more worse could this house arrest be? My little girls though were displaying amazing fortitude. I grumpily said I was not squatting down anymore to pick up the ball at every hole. You do it. My knees hurt. My eldest looked up at me and sighed inwardly. The resigned expression on her little face said, "I am stuck with this cranky old bat for the rest of my life," but still she patiently humoured me. Hey, apparently there were some advantages to having kids. Like when you don't want to squat.

Before we knew it, it was 6pm.

Day 5 of Circuit Breaker had ended.

* * *

Here's some appreciation for teachers. Thank you for keeping our kids alive in the day and thank you for educating our kids. If we don't say it enough, thank you so so much.

[Standing ovation]

Motherhood is the Greatest Job
You'll Ever Fxxx Up

"Anything you can imagine, you can create," is a quote by Oprah Winfrey, soon to be President of the United States.

"A child?" my answer was.

"If you try hard enough," a friend replied.

He must have meant to make them disappear, instead of making more of them. In the meantime, an all too familiar scene was forming at my dining table.

Prior to that Facebook banter with a friend, I had just made a discreet amendment in my kids' suggested timetables for Home Based Learning (HBL) that day, swapping Mathematics for

Mindfulness, as I no longer had the wherewithal to do anymore fractions or probabilities of Jane the Zookeeper picking a parrot out of an imaginary bag full of random animals. Surreptitiously so.

The timetables were covered with correction tapes, two or three layers for each cell. As we, parents, i.e. horrible substitute teachers, were given the authority to change the suggested subjects for the day as we saw fit. Evidently I changed my mind as the hour progressed each day according to which academic vexations I could endure for the day.

Last night, in an attempt to better myself as a parent on lockdown, I read Tony Robbins' empowering note regarding the power of words. I had written a brief note to self: "Transformational vocabulary regarding the lockdown: from 'absolutely brutal' to a 'smite inconvenient'. Starting tomorrow."

"I am a Firewalker!" read his seminar's certificate staring back at me on my bedroom bed stand. It felt more like a mockery at this moment, that I could conquer and achieve anything I put my mind to. That seminar last year felt like a lifetime ago.

To illustrate, the HBL principal actors involved:

Sophia, 9 years old, Primary 4.

Sabrina, 6 years old, Primary 2.

Me = Exhausted Mum, 100 years old.

The standoff of at the dining table unfolded as follows.

Sabrina: "Sophia is always bullying me!" Arms crossed, hiding under the table. My sensitive little one. Earlier in the week her first tooth had fallen out and the little creature got even more sensitive, body and soul.

Sophia, chuckling dismissively: "I did not! I was just trying to teach her how to read the clock!"

Exhausted mum: "Sophia, you mean old thing. That's it. No more ipad for you."

Sophia: "Oh? That's not fair. I was just trying to help!"

Exhausted mum: "Well did she ask for your help?"

Sophia (couldn't hide a cheeky little glint in her eyes): "No."

Mum: "Then what happened?"

Sophia: "Well, her Math homework disappeared from Studyladder. But we could do it again! It's so easy."

My Little Miss Know It All. God did have a sense of humour. If we thought ourselves so fabulous, let's see if we are gifted with a little clone of 'us' in the world, a little mirror, so to speak. Let's see if we still thought ourselves fabulous then.

The incident rather reminded me of my brother and I when I used to whisper to him (when he was a toddler) that a spider had fallen into his crib. It's ok. After all the imaginary spider ordeal I tortured him with, he turned to martial arts for self defence. With a flick of his wrist he could now defend himself and all of us against anything that walked or crawled, collecting black belts in all forms of martial arts imaginable. See, things did turn out well, even if a little extreme.

My little one started to scream. "Sophia's always bullying me!" No new information there. Such promising, piercing high notes, but it's making me deaf now. The irony of my lifetime pursuit on high notes. "How high could you go," doesn't it run in the family? But as of today, this penchant of hereditary melodrama was getting old.

Older sister was still grinning.

Me: "Now, I don't know how you're going to do it, but you make her stop. You sort this out. Otherwise you know she's going to cry for one whole hour."

Sophia shrugged her shoulders, and reluctantly coaxed her bawling sister from under the table.

Fast forward to bedtime. Peeped at them from the door crack. They were hugging each other to sleep.

"I love you, Sophia."

"I love you too, sis."

Sisters, a lifetime of love and hate. I told each of them that your sister is your friend for life.

I had enrolled them both for a survival swimming course. Sophia had completed her course early, and so brilliantly. Her video went viral as a three-year-old that could not sink. She was hopeless at ballet but had always been very sporty. Currently, she was the reigning Queen of Freestyle for inter-school swim meets for her age group, despite her petite stature. The sister, Sabrina, was taught how to float from an early age too, but the exercise always became a Titanic sinking episode on account of her hair. She had always been very preoccupied about her hair and looks in general, and with survival swimming for some reason her hair always got in her face. I wasn't aware enough to put on a cap then, but then it was supposed to simulate a real life accidental fall into a pool with clothes and shoes on anyway. I didn't expect this to change much in adulthood. But coming back to swimming, Sophia had pep-talked her sister by the pool when Sabrina did her test. The aim was for her to achieve a starfish-like pose, face up, floating in water, within seconds of being thrown into the water. She was doing well until she fussed with her hair and started sinking. Sophia yelled, "Sabrina! Get your hands out! Hands out on your sides! Stop fussing with your hair!" To no avail. The Little Titanic went under again.

Sisters also knew how to push each other's buttons like no other. The little (passive aggressive) one knew how to tailor her words as such so as to piss off her eldest sister with maximum impact. All she needed to say was a slinky, almost undetectable "Oh, look at her. Sophia is a little bit upset, Mum." And that would send her eldest sister jumping up and down in frenzy, ending up with her usual, "I don't want a sister! Why did you give me a sister, she is so annoying! I want a brother!"

With regards to her having a brother in any distant future, I did express to all suitors concerned that I am open to the possibility of having more children, with some persuasion. But that idea has been drastically revised thanks to this Home Based Learning on lockdown. Whatever additional children I desired next would come out of Toys R Us, and would be made of plastic. I shall issue the necessary proclamation in due course, unless convinced otherwise.

Back to sisters. They might not always see eye to eye, but you cross one, you cross both. Shortly before the lockdown there was an accusation that my little girl had been bullied. Oh horror! Bullied!

Being an enlightened (I was not on house arrest then so I was quite right in the head still) yet slightly alarmed single mum, I decided not to jump to conclusions and not do my usual turning up at school upon a whiff of such news.

I sent the older sister to investigate the situation. What exactly happened? It would be good problem solving and life skills for her too, I thought. I told her to be diplomatic and not make it worse. Just pay the little human beings a visit and find out things.

I reckoned maybe take a break from my helicopter parenting for a change and let's see how they resolve this problem. Although secretly I was sending a powerful envoy with a war message that this little bleating creature had a much older, big sister. A bodyguard in school. That should sort things out. My bigger girl seemed to feel strongly about that too. Nobody else was allowed to bully her sister other than her.

One day that week, Sophia came home looking very pleased with herself.

"I've sorted it out, Mum. It's settled. There is no problem now."

I enquired curiously, what happened, what did she do.

She did pay the little kids a visit. "Hi. I'm Sabrina's sister. I'm in Year 4."

Old, so old. must have been bloody scary for the little ones. "I heard you bullied my sister," said Sophia to the alleged bully, who turned out to be a little girl cherub with golden ringlets.

"Can you tell me what happened? By the way, you see that boy there? (indicating a tall boy walking to and fro in a horizontal line, from one end of the school canteen to the other end, carrying a soccer ball). He is my best friend."

Wonder if you all recall that when we were very young kids, even a year difference seemed like so much. The older kids, they all seemed so big, so knowledgeable, so tall and scary. Knowing a more senior student if even by a year older was so cool. They had everything figured out, yes they did. Until they all went to college and sniffed drugs or got pregnant.

Sophia had brought reinforcement. She herself was apparently quite apprehensive at the prospect of having to confront and be surrounded by possibly legions of even smaller little people. The bodyguard had brought a bodyguard. And that reinforcement was none other than one of her best friends in class, a boy who was the tallest and biggest kid in their year. They didn't know he was a gentle giant. She had told him to follow her to the school canteen during recess, and to walk from one end of the canteen, to the other, and not to stop doing so until she gave a sign. The boy was none the wiser until this day.

The cherub in ringlets was admirably courageous. She replied in a matter of fact manner to my big girl, "Your sister said my singing was bad. She laughed at me. So I called her poopypants."

Oh, boy. A facepalm moment. My angel, my little saint, was the bully. I was mortified. Thank God I didn't turn up at school and throw my miserable weight about. I asked though, what was it that the other girl was singing. They said it was Elsa's *Let It Go* from the old *Frozen* movie. Of course it was.

I commended my eldest girl on her first successful diplomatic mission, then proceeded to give my little girl a lecture, that when you hear people singing flat you should not tell them their singing is terrible. They would not want to be your friend.

"So I should not tell them the truth then?"

"No, see, (me, grappling for the right words), if you cannot find anything nice to say about people (or their singing), then just don't say anything. Say something nice about them that is true."

"Oh. Ok, Mummy. But it's ok we are friends now, we played together at school today."

Children's friendship were ever so fluid. Don't we all wish we could be like children. But sometimes it is our children who teach us many things. Especially when we're locked up 24/7 with them for months on end.

Pure enlightenment.

HBL + WFH = WTF

"Mum, you look drowsy. Why are you sitting around on the sofa with a coffee cup? Don't be lazy."

It was Week 2 of the horrendous, treacherous era called Home Based Learning (HBL). I had aged a decade in one week. There were security issues they said with the real-time video streaming platform. So surprise, surprise. Guess who was school teacher for the month. I am a single mum. So it's just me, myself, and I.

"Lazy…? WHAT DID YOU SAY? I'M LAZY?! Come back here you little twerp! I'll put you back inside me!! You little @#$%^ BLA BLA BLA BLA BLA…"

These were the children we were all killing ourselves to have.

I had taken a momentary pause between the subjects of Art (I couldn't draw to save my life) and French (which I had to Google).

I was so exhausted and so were the rest of the mothers in the world too. I was so tired that I accidentally swallowed a small insect floating in my tea, and only realised after.

I hoped it did not have COVID-19. Oh bloody hell. For those who do not have children, please close your eyes and imagine.

Remember when your dad tried teaching you how to drive? And started shouting at you to brake at the top of his lungs even though the rubbish bin was still 50 metres away? And then you enrolled at the driving school and that's how you were able to drive now? Yep, that was it. Keep that thought in mind.

It is never a good idea to teach one's own kid.

"CALL ME LAZY ONE MORE TIME AND I'LL MAKE JAWS (THE SHARK) LOOK LIKE PINK FAIRY FLOSS!" I roared.

The little troll ran away giggling.

Seriously, if she didn't come out of me, if I hadn't thrown up six times a day for six months when she was in my belly, if she hadn't sucked the living life out of me (literally) for two years while I was breastfeeding her and if her face hadn't looked so much like my own, I would have strangled her. What an ungrateful little imp! Arrghhh!

I had a mutually beneficial venting session at night with a fellow tired Mum and we both couldn't agree more, if only we had dared to speak like that to our parents! Oh! "Someone's gonna get hurt!" (do-mi-so sing-song tone). Cane, belt or broom? Please choose your tool of choice. That's how we rolled in our days eh! Now, they say we have to reason with these little humans. REASON. It's an unreasonable request. Since it was no longer fashionable to beat the crap out of our kids these days, I did what I did best. I yelled.

Hey before Coronavirus, I actually got paid to yell, without amplification, so long as it resembled a combination of coherent notes. These little trolls got it for free. They ought to be grateful, no? You want octaves? I'll give you octaves! Especially if I had to Home School for another month or so, or God forbid, the rest of the year.

It worked for the most part. And for some reason the kids found me funny, even when I yelled. I must have done something wrong. I need to ask around for tips what was it I did wrong.

I had taught, supervised, planned and bloody documented seven to nine subjects daily, times two. And I had uploaded more photos and videos to poor teachers than I cared to count in a lifetime.

At least today it was uploaded to the correct platform. Before that I didn't realise I was spamming the rest of the class. I was a dinosaur, a true Mum-REX.

My six-year old's teacher said we were to present two or three works each week. Today I uploaded nine. Yes, had to be *kiasu, lah* (i.e.

Singaporean term similar to English urban slang FOMO. Such as when parents enrolled kids in all manner of tuition to get ahead). My kids must get on in life, I vowed. They must do well. And look what I got in return.

Yesterday was utterly absurd. None of the platforms for online learning worked. I could not upload anything properly, or maybe it was just me. Today the three platforms did perform their tasks as I had spammed the classroom teachers for pointers. I don't know how they do this for a living. Gosh I think they deserve this month's 'break'. They must all be cooking and trying out new dishes in confinement.

I had sneaked off to do my CALM app in the toilet, chanting to myself, "I am calm. I am calm. I am calm," to infinity. But they found me. RAP, RAP, RAP, on the toilet door.

"Mum, what are you doing? I don't hear any water. I need you to help me with my work. It needs more words."

"GO AWAY. I'm in the toilet and don't come in here!" (Can you believe that they knew how to pick the lock from the outside.)

"It is not polite to barge in while people are sitting in the toilet. I'll be out in a moment!!" I continued.

You want words? I'll give you words! I bellowed inwardly, brandishing my fangs. Home Based Learning. Yes, a learning curve for parents to teach us patience and not to outsource it.

Today while I was painstakingly typing a short accompanying report for her French lesson (before uploading it to the supposedly very user friendly platform), "*Lessss monggg...duh trevailll...*" (Ahem. I sing in French, not speak). My little one interjected with a knowing, little smile.

"Mum, that's not how you say it."

"Eh? Then how?"

"*Les monde du travail.* Not too much Ssssss. "

In an effortless, perfect, uninterrupted French. How could this creature who just three years ago was hanging off my boobs be speaking with a perfect French accent? Well you know those smart researchers say that children's brains were like sponges at this age. I had read a 500-page 'easy read' guide for parents written by scientists on this topic. The gist of it was as such. How true. I better not swear so much.

The rest of the subjects today, I admit I did digress a little from the teachers' instructions, taking some artistic liberties along the way.

Performing Arts. Ballet Practice.

Visual Arts. She made necklaces and Lego.

Music. I fudged and pretended her online piano lesson was just her learning from an app. I submitted a photo, not video this time. The teacher gave a standard reply, "Good job." Sometimes it was just a heart. I'm happy when I receive a two-word reply.

French. I used an app.

Mandarin. Ah! A little more effort here, from a website!

Maths. God bless whoever invented *Studyladder*.

English. I should have stuck to the earlier study plan of them reading to self, but I made the mistake of suggesting to my eldest that she should dissect the story of *The Secret Garden*. *Alamak,* an essay. Me and my big mouth.

P.E. Replaced with Mindfulness today, this topic is all the craze these days. They fell asleep for 15 minutes. Fantastic. The best thing ever.

Unit Of Inquiry (UOI). This was a research project to explore a given topic. We actually had to do some real work. As in I had to do some real work. I spent three bloody hours doing up her presentation on Apple's Keynote. Next week it would be a sheet of paper, handwritten. That's it. We're going manual.

My Mothers WhatsApp Group had been pinging this afternoon. Not so much for exchange of information but more like an emotional support group for all of us in the same boat. One mother today had to retrieve all three of her children out of her husband's 'home office' while he was on teleconference with the office. Similar to the BBC dad who went viral on the internet, except this fellow mum had her pants around her ankles. She had to rush out from the toilet in that state. I was sharing my meditation in the toilet situation and she said I was lucky to even be able to go to the toilet. Poor lady. See, the number of kids and the problems they cause do not go in linear proportion. It is exponential. It does not mean two kids equals problems x two, and three kids is problems x three. No, no, no. It is not quite like that. Exponential, I said. It is to the power of.

HBL under lockdown or quarantine, is quintessentially Jurassic Park of the 21st century.

Another mother's experience. Whenever she asked her boys to do their work, they'd say yes demurely with a smile, but continued not to do any work.

She had to write bullet point house rules for her boys:

- You may not call mummy useless
- During meal times, eat whatever is in front of you
- If mummy says do it, then just do it.

Nike got the right slogan, don't they.

As part of her Shakespearean outrage this afternoon (with regards to the unicorn game they refused to budge from): "Life is not all popcorn or unicorn!"

She said she realised immediately after that outburst, she did not know why she included popcorn in her angry recitative, so she just turned around and stormed off to drill her point across.

I told her I was doing well until 8pm today.

She replied, "8pm? Please share your tip on how to last until 8pm."

I tried to comfort her and said at least she got a smile. We gave each other virtual hugs and parted ways to face another battle the next day.

Meanwhile somewhere in Australia: "I am so exhausted. So exhausted! I could only work starting at 7.30pm when he goes to bed! And he's only in kindergarten!" said my friend Michelle, a Filipina investment banker married to a Jewish IT specialist.

"You know they gave me these guidelines, and today I had to research stones. They're going to go bushwalking, you see, these Australians. Like I care about the different kinds of stones! For a 5-year-old!!" she continued.

"It was full on, from 9am all the way to 3.30pm! No effin' break!" she continued.

"Hmmmhmmm. I hear you, I hear you.." I quipped.

"I thought we were doing mighty well, until the teacher asked, 'Are you guys three modules behind?'"

Michelle is the go-getter sort and naturally she put her son in a top, expensive private school. Apparently the amount of Home Based Learning, or, Distance Learning, as they called it there, was commensurate. Wouldn't want the parents to feel they didn't get value for their money, would they?

Infuriated, she wanted to throw the laptop on the floor, but there was the teacher on video conference smiling at her. Michelle had to smile back.

"Babe, seriously, I don't know how people do it," she moaned.

It's bad enough we had to be unpaid school teachers, but some of us, actually had to Work From Home. Those whose jobs were not considered essential, such as (but not limited to) musicians, artists, restaurateurs, health instructors, business owners, authors and so many others. It was a necessary measure, but not without pain.

Funny though how suddenly while under House Arrest, our kids' timetables suddenly burgeoned with the so-called least appreciated subjects, like Art, Music and P.E. These were the professions considered unessential enough to be excluded from most government funding during this dire time. Well as we discovered, it was certainly essential to keep us sane at this time.

As the icing on the cake, in Singapore we live in apartments, or at least most of us peasants do. A 150 square metre space, with three bedrooms, was already considered generous by today's standards. It really did impose an impossible selection of space, for all these activities to take place altogether in the same dwelling.

I lived in a 2 bedroom flat. My configurations:

Kid #1: dining table

Kid #2: living room

Domestic helper: second bedroom

Me: A small makeshift corner in main bedroom enough for a laptop on my vanity table and an Ikea chair.

I wondered how the other parents did it. I did not have to wonder long.

My friend Martin was relegated to the bathroom. He had a rather spirited set of twin toddlers and had to go on conference calls all day. Meanwhile my friend Ben, living on the other side of the island, victoriously took possession of the kitchen. It had a door. His current office was between the dustbin and the sink.

These were just some of the crazy family issues we all faced during the live saving Circuit Breaker, or lockdown, or Movement Control Order, as some others would call it.

Well a wise woman once said, "It may take a village to raise a child, but it takes a vineyard to homeschool one."

[*POP!*]

[Bottle opened].

And the Horror Based Learning Continues

"I drink, and I know things," said Tyrion Lannister in *Game of Thrones*. Of all the quotes of wise men I could come up with, at this time, none be the wiser.

One month into the wretched HBL (Home Based Learning).

HBL in the daytime, plus me writing in the night 'til the wee hours of the morning, for it was the only time when the dining table was mine, all mine. These combined labours to be executed while being locked up (or down, whatever you prefer), were perhaps one of the hardest things I'd ever done, next to my much earlier job of keeping the same little human beings alive with my boobs.

You know when they say that men have a nothing box in their brain? (i.e. a box that contains nothing, in case the phrase was not self explanatory enough). I was starting to have a nothing box too.

"I - got - nothing" (rotating my head and shaking it).

After one month, my self-imposed expectations had been lowered. And I meant low. Soon I would be one of those parents who taught life skills such as living room camping.

This morning as I headed for the toilet, the kids asked, "Mum? Where are you going? Are you coming back?"

No, I'm not coming back. I will camp in the toilet for the rest of my life. Look, these schools have got to open, otherwise we parents would start a riot very soon.

And then, "Mum! How do I log in to Google Meet?"

Me, calling out from the toilet, "Just Google it!"

To make matters worse, the kids' laptop decided to die in a most opportunistic manner this weekend. Just before the first day of the school's new format of live video conferencing.

I was tidying up their folders of past work and reviewing their work for the following week (so Monday would not become too panic-ridden), when the wretched device decided to pull a Sleeping Beauty on me. The screen remained stubbornly dark. I could hear that it was whirring, but it remained asleep. How cheeky. I wished I was asleep. But I could not recall when was the last time I was asleep this month. Like really asleep.

There I was, spamming teachers for help for the 15th time on all given platforms imaginable.

Upon my frantic visit to the service centre, I was advised that someone must have dropped some liquid on it. Corrosion, the technician said. It came back alive but not sure for how long. Corrosion was not the word you wanted to hear. Corrosion was expensive.

I hoped it would remain alive for at least a month during the purport remaining of this lockdown.

Hence the start of my in-house misadventures for the second month of lockdown.

Just the weekend before, the school decided to change the format, upon some parents' complaints of lack of face-to-face time between teachers and students. Geez thanks, see what happened to us now?

Starting the following Monday onwards, at 9am sharp, they would have bloody HBL via video-conference. Three times a day of check-ins, for each kid. Which meant parents had got to have their shit in order by 9am and had to be perky and chirpy by the kids' side, to assist on everything they needed. Or else your kid won't get marked for attendance. I discovered soon enough that this new initiative was not mainly used for teaching. It was to keep us on our toes, since we complained so much. These video conferences were to say hi, and to check if we were asleep.

Now, the teachers (as we discovered) were national heroes, for putting up with our kids all day all year round. I noticed that they too were starting to run out of ideas on how to keep distance learning stimulating.

Cats started to make cameo appearances at the teachers' morning videos. And then baking, and more baking.

First it was the Chicken Dance. And then there came the very meaningful Toilet Paper Challenge. I must say Singaporeans did very well at this last challenge, look at all the empty aisles in the supermarkets, whilst the home teaching of subjects, have evolved as such.

Let's start with Mathematics.

Tessellation? What on earth is a tessellation? Does anyone know? I don't think they called it tessellation in my time. Somebody must have invented that word to sound smart between now and the time that we were in school.

"You mean translation?" I asked my nine-year-old with a blank face, her little face looking up at me expectantly.

Now don't even get me started on Math story problems as I had problems!

They went along the lines of, "Jane has 5 dogs, 2 birds, 2 chimpanzees and 3 giraffes at home. What is the probability for Jane to grab a bird out of this lot, when blindfolded?"

Jane must have been a zookeeper. Probability of my going insane? 100%.

Subject: P.E.

Juggling for P.E. Was she supposed to make a living juggling? According to the teacher, there were four steps to juggling. You used two balls or socks. Up and down, and up and down, and up. Then down. I was to record all these flying socks on camera, for marking.

Whilst on the module, "to train kids' gross motor skills," we had to train them to catch a ball. I never, ever, could catch a ball in my entire life. It always landed flat on my face, especially during volleyball practice in school. Sorry but there was not the slightest hope of me ever teaching them that.

I reckoned a better use of my kids' time on the subject of P.E. was to practise massage, on mum. A very good practice of motor skills. If all else failed, a fairly legit money making profession too.

Kids noticed this afternoon that mum had studied most intently, Behind-the-Scenes Aquaman's exercise videos while standing up. She moved absentmindedly to her chair, with her eyes still glued to the screen, and missed it completely, landing flat on her bottom on the floor.

Subject: English Language.

For the whole month we had been writing poems. I was so over poems. Especially when they were about the environment and renewable energy. Who on earth wrote poems on those topics, one might wonder aloud. Oh but trust me, there were.

Today for a change, I had to explain a highly technical term.

"Mum, what is 'declined'?"

"Declined is when you don't wanna do something. Or when your credit card won't work when you swipe in the store."

This HBL was making me a retard. So much for being a writer. I didn't have words anymore.

"Sophia, eat your broccoli."

"Declined." What a smartass I've created. Ok.

"When a boy asks you to kiss him, what do you say??"

Both girls, cheekily in unison, "DECLINED!!"

At least I did something right there. Here's hoping they will say 'declined' at least until they enter university. All parents' wistful thinking.

And then, other than having to explain to them this week's topic of, "Social Skills Kids Need" (they forgot to insert, 'In Quarantine'), God forbid, the subject was French.

"*Le jours de la semaine.*" The little one was to say it aloud and memorise the days of the week. As in me, repeating it aloud for an hour with the aid of whatever was available online. But wait a minute, what day was it today?

"*Semaine,* not cement," her know-it-all elder sister cut in from across the dining table, behind her laptop.

French? I know French. *Chateaunef du Pape.* That will comprise of: French + History + Religion (it's the Catholics again) + Botany (on grapes) + Life Skill (uncorking a bottle). Wouldn't it? Talk about killing a few birds with one stone.

For Art, we had to make puppets that week. I decided swiftly on a toilet-roll puppet (as it was the easiest). I discovered I only had one toilet roll which I fished out of the bin and disinfected. Because that was the only kind of puppet I knew how to make. I just needed to shit more and faster so we had more toilet roll cardboards, to make more puppets with.

Time for a late morning tea break! Off I went to the kitchen. These days, beverages of choice to accompany HBL being:

Morning: free-flow coffee.

Daytime: officially coffee. Well, somebody somewhere (guess who) was hellbent on trying to prove that I was an alcoholic PLUS crazy (or, 'possessed by evil spirits every Tuesday', in his claim). Crazy was great, if you're a Crazy Rich Asian. But if you're just crazy, plus Asian? Not so. But I must say the crazy part was getting pretty close to the mark at this rate.

Evening: officially wine or beer, or whatever sedatives I could find in my pantry. Alcoholic? Definitely maybe.

Most nights though, I cheated on these old faithfuls with a nice cup of green or chamomile tea with biscuits. Very Anglophile. Damn, it must be old age. I would never admit this to friends.

After that brief trip to the kitchen, I settled back on my seat. The next subject on the timetable, was one hour of 'Manipulative Play'. I couldn't help but laugh, and wondered if other parents did too.

Are we to teach children to be manipulative at a young age? Or worse, the 'play' connotation. Yes my mind is in the gutter. Then I learned what it was.

Time to phone a friend! Not currently a parent (or at least none that he knew of), "When I say 'manipulative play', what comes to your mind?"

"Emotional manipulation."

"It was actually when you put out toys in front of kids, and let them play with it. Like building blocks or clay to develop their specific motor skills. The opposite is Free Play meaning to let them play with whatever they want."

During that night's conversation I bombarded him with all sorts of unrelated random questions, as my mind had... nothing. It was just full of nothing boxes.

"Is this quiz some kind of Rorschach test?"

"Rosh... what?"

"It's the inkblot test. They show you a bunch of inkblots. You tell them what they meant. Then they decide whether you are nuts."

"Hmmmm. Maybe I should be doing that test. Oh wait. I did that test!"

"(Worried for himself) Do I want to know why?"

"Was it those funny tests on Facebook asking you if you could see other shapes other than the obvious? I always see the other shapes. Does that mean I'm crazy?"

My friend concluded by saying he's not a nut doctor but in any case last time he checked I had enough control of my faculties. Enough to fill up my whole trolley with Indomie instant noodles at the supermarket before the lockdown. Who cared about toilet paper? I'd choose stomach over backside any day.

I then accidentally sent the guy a unicorn.

"Sorry, typo. Wasn't meant to send you unicorns."

So much for motor skills.

For now, time to upload my submission for the Mother-Daughter Chicken Dance Competition.

Happy Hour!

Setting: At home in the time of the Global Quarantine. It was to be a whole month, which became nearly three, of Happy Hour, seven days a week in most households.

Now, imagine a circus. Close your eyes. You hear the ringmaster's booming voice.

"On top of the list, parents! Coming up next, pretty much neck to neck with parents, are teachers! Thank you. Clap clap clap.

And then we have [drum roll], single bored people!

Right behind them, Christians and Atheists!

And finally [announced very quickly in a sequence [drum roll] men, women, anything-in-between and all manner of frustrated people!"

Basically a lot of people. You may open your eyes now. With all the travel restrictions in place, people's option to connect with other people was limited to tablets at home. Aided with drinks, one got to travel to other places, at least in one's own mind. Everything became possible, and with more drinks, everyone looked better.

Here are some real accounts of live video-conference travels:

ACT 1, SCENE 1. Houseparty. Living Room.

9.30pm. 1 red, 1 white, 1 whisky.

"What was that?" I was so confused. A crooked line emerged clumsily on the screen in front of us. It was starting to resemble a familiar reproductive apparatus we all knew. On the previous round I guessed correctly that Barrack Obama was considered 'Overrated' according to the app's playing cards. Wonder what the cards would say about Trump in that case.

"..............."

"It's a d*ck," Amir deduced flatly.

BEEP! Time's up. Zero points for all of us in this round of charades.

"It's a vacuum cleaner, you guys," an exasperated Charlie announced from his end.

Either we sucked (no pun intended) or Charlie was just bad at drawing.

Amir seemed to be doing very well in the earlier rounds on pop culture. Suspiciously so. He even guessed correctly Alyssa Milano's witch role in *Charm* the TV series from the 90s.

Nobody could answer anything out of the Heavy Metal category. Everyone also had mediocre General Knowledge but did quite well on All About Animals.

An hour of quizzes and drawings later we said our goodbyes, after a short intermezzo of Amir's mum phoning in (heard on speakerphone) to check if he wore a mask or left it at home this time when he went to the grocery store. Another wrap-up of the usual Happy Hour at my place.

ACT 1, SCENE 2. WhatsApp video call. Location: sitting on the floor behind my barricaded bedroom door, and hiding from kids.

7pm. Beer versus wine.

"What time is Happy Hour at your place?"

"Starts at 4pm to pretty much 8pm, daily. 8pm is when he needs to go to bed. Normally I'd lock myself up and say 'Mummy has to work, which means I go to my 'home office' and browse YouTube or Lazada for four hours and occasionally reply a few emails. So long as I emerge from my 'office' by 8pm, all is well," my friend said.

Smile. My Katharina was the best. P.S. 4pm is when home school wraps up most days.

Earlier on I was texting with another mum and she shared that hers started at noon on weekdays. She has three kids, hence, definitely Happy Hour from noon.

I opted for After Hours Happy Hour which meant it's 9pm onwards. At least I didn't have to pour my beer into a unicorn plastic cup meant for apple juice. I was slightly traditional. Must be my parents. It has been three decades and their painfully pious voices never left my head.

ACT 1, SCENE 3. Facetime. Location: between my kitchen and the living room, while kids after school were busy in conversation with friends in their own room.

5pm. Hard liquor of indefinite origin versus coffee. Guess which one was mine. I was finishing my third cup for the day in a bid to stay awake.

Those were the familiar cases. In some other homes, the quarantine might very well be an all-day Happy Hour. These were single people who also happened to be too rich to work. Trust me there was such a breed. Don't hate them. Befriend them.

"Happy Hour, Babe!"

"Happy indeed!" I had just finished HBL for the day and it felt like I just got home from a war with camels and got spat on all over.

"Now, now. Tell Papa J what's up."

"Nothing is up, Jamie. Everything is down. It's been a drought, thank you. But yeah, tell me."

"A guy seized the opportunity when people were not in the office and took some money. He actually wrote a note that he would return it. It's like $50,000."

Obviously the dude hadn't returned Jamie's office money, hence the free shrink session.

ACT 2, SCENE 1. Zoom Group Video Call. Location: master bedroom.

In case you're wondering, I just wrote it as ACT 2 because operas normally have three scenes in each act. Unless it's Wagner in which case after three hours you'd sleep, you'd wake up, then you'd fall asleep again, and the next time you open your eyes the next day, they were still singing.

10.30pm. Some Austrian hard liquor versus miscellaneous beers plus Baileys.

"Today is the day I put my husband up for sale," my friend from Austria announced. Apparently she had fed him seven times that day and he still wanted more food, prepared by her.

Another lady friend quipped, "Quarantine Day 47, will pay if you take my husband!"

"I wanted to sell him long ago. How can I wait until Day 47??"

Men and women stuck 24/7 at home were tethering on the territory of Not So Happy Hour.

This lockdown seemed to bring about the most aggravating domestic issues between men and women. They could only bonk so many times a day, so for the rest of the hours they actually had to talk and be normal. Do chores. Get along.

It has been proven by science that men on average can regurgitate 7,000 words a day, whereas women, a whopping 20,000 words. I read it somewhere. But hey, having said that, that did not seem to be a level playing field for the men stuck at home.

ACT 2, SCENE 2. Zoom Work Conference Call. Location: living room.

9.30pm. The commonly agreed time as the most civilised hour for Happy Hour. Too many varieties of drinks to list.

An actual meeting to discuss the future of our postponed opera production with 12 participants. Imagine everyone from director to composer to stage director to cast members, taking a swig every few uncoordinated seconds and put that collective Zoom frame on double time with a Mexican Mariachi as background music. A stunning sight.

ACT 3, THE FINALE. House party. Location: living room.

9.30 pm. Wines. My good friends with kids have a Happy Hour every Friday to celebrate surviving another week of HBL.

"Hello, hello."

"Hey, everyone!"

"This remote learning really sucks, man," said a single dad. Second time lucky.

A million cheers later and even more failures in guessing all the charades and quizzes the app provided, we concluded that we were perhaps the wrong generation for these games. But it was indeed very nice to catch up and spend our Happy Hour with friends this way.

* * *

A quiet thought. It only took a mere global pandemic for us to use communication devices as those devices ought to be used.

May that obsession with that spellbinding glassy abyss while loved ones are about, be a thing of the past. Once we were safely let out of our enclosures.

Lest we forget.

ON FRIENDSHIP & OTHER ISSUES

In Eggs We Trust

Harriet's sister, Muriel, had explicitly told her not to give her son Noah any Easter eggs this year. Harriet of course did not listen. Harriet was the older sister, in the physical sense of the word.

Harriet didn't listen when her sister warned her against the danger of wearing 14cm high platform shoes while climbing up the stairs in a cinema. Her sister had also advised against picking Row A for seats, seeing as they were both in unrealistically elevated high heels which were the trend then.

They had gone into the cinema 30 minutes late. The movie was *The English Patient.* It was ok, Ralph Fiennes died much later in the movie. As they were groping around in the dark, making their way up the stairs, Harriet lost her balance and grabbed her sister who was one step ahead, and they both went humpty dumpty down the cinema stairs in their mini-skirts. Not the most preferable entrance. But it was somewhat ok as it was in the dark, and they had both crawled up on all fours to the top row. Muriel has only worn flats since then.

Every Easter, the family would congregate at Harriet's, she being the eldest child. As a very good host Harriet always made sure everyone, be they family or friends (sometimes foe), emerged out her door with their stomachs (very) full.

Not so this year. Coronavirus, the ugly step-sister of SARS came to visit. All had to remain at home. Furthermore, Harriet, being a lab rat, needed to self-isolate from others as she was the one doing the testing for the actual Coronavirus.

Before the time of Coronavirus, she conducted tests for all sorts of things, from the flu (boring) to STDs (not boring). I asked if she ever came across familiar names, perhaps of her Ex, and/or mine. What wouldn't I give to make some people lose sleep for one more night.

"Do you think one might be mistakenly tested positive for, say syphilis?"

"Yeah, and I could throw in gonorrhea free of charge."

She said she could not disclose anything, but a false positive could always happen to anyone, and be corrected approximately one or two sleepless weeks later. This is why one must try to be nice to everyone. You'd never know who would be doing your STD testing.

Harriet marched into her neighbourhood store to purchase Easter eggs for her nephew. But even the Easter eggs supply these days were affected. There were only bunnies, and one box of Easter eggs in a dimly lit corner. The packaging was shaped like a walking stick with a funny pointed end. It had a hollow in the middle filled with six Easter eggs, arranged vertically. Perhaps it was the wrong season, or there was an oversupply of these weirdly shaped containers. It must have been rejected goods and they just wanted to clear up their inventory.

Let's put it this way, it looked like a certain male apparatus filled with eggs, Harriet told me over the phone. But she was running late and she didn't want to go to another store and risk being left empty-handed so she grabbed it and went to the till. Who cared about the packaging, so long as there were eggs.

She mused how every year she had organised an Easter egg hunt in the garden for her son as he was growing up. It never ended well. The bees one time, another time he had got stuck in one of the low hedges. Her son was most relieved when he came of age and this painful tradition came to an end.

Harriet then turned her attention to her beloved little nephew, to carry on this scavenger hunt legacy.

I told her our Easter egg hunt in this lockdown year was just within the flat. Unfortunately at our age, we can hide the Easter eggs, wait half an hour, and have no clue where we put them. So when my kids couldn't find the remaining eggs, there I was joining in the scavenger hunt along with them, for real.

Harriet decided to take public transport that day and she dragged her teenage son along. She had that tube of eggs firmly cradled under her arm. Not a good look. All the way from the bus ride to her sister's place. She would not meet them, instead she would find a way to pass her Easter present and eggs, and leave.

She stopped two bus stops too early. Harriet normally drove but that day she fancied doing something different and had worn her active wear (barely used previously) to complete the look.

She travelled on foot with the eggs and her son for the rest of the three blocks. They passed a church backyard, where a startled priest was watering the plants, passed a stadium, and a park where people were 'social distancing' (i.e. picnic disguised as exercise). In case she was questioned as to why she and her son were out and about, she was prepared to flash her 'essential worker' card.

It was a good half-hour walk. People were staring at her, and her pointy golden eggs. Her son had actually walked a few steps behind. Harriet slowly realised that she was attracting attention for the wrong reason, so she turned around and asked her son if he would carry the eggs instead in exchange for some present.

He said, "No thanks Mum, I'd take cash this year."

They arrived at Muriel's place. Her flat was on the first floor. It came with a personal private space with a fence just above Harriet's head (Harriet was not a massive woman). Her sister and brother-in-law were nowhere in sight, but lo and behold, the glass door was slightly opened and her little toddler nephew hobbled through the door. Harriet called out to him. He recognised her happily.

"You want eggs? Aunt Harriet has got some eggs for you," in a singsong baby talk.

Her son rolled his eyes.

Harriet proceeded to open the packaging and took out the first golden egg. She attempted to throw it over the fence. Social distancing, you see. Not supposed to meet.

The first egg grazed the top of her nephew's head. Her son, horrified, exclaimed, "Mum! Don't injure the boy!"

Harriet paid no heed. Five more eggs to go. Off she jumped to throw another egg.

"Ooo little koochy-koo! Catch!"

It landed far away in a corner somewhere.

"Rats!" she swore under her breath. She had failed P.E. in school.

Two more attempts with eggs brushing either side of the poor little tot's head. This was a pointless exercise as she could not throw and the boy was a moving target. He didn't cry though, he was too excited jumping around trying to catch these golden eggs that fell from the sky. Her son had screamed, "Watch out!!" on the last two throws.

"Mum, you're a hopeless egg thrower. Look, I'll do it." her son offered.

Harriet, a little peeved, replied testily, "It's not my problem he's got butter fingers."

Her son implored her to give it up. "Look, Mum, don't throw it. Just try wriggling it over the top of the fence, very closely so it rolled down nicely against the inside of the fence."

How's that for some engineering slash physics? Why didn't he think of that earlier, Harriet thought. The eggs were rather soft by then, having been dragged across town, and they came down with a splat. Some cleaning for Muriel to do there.

For the finalé, there was the present. Her son, fearing for the little boy's life, insisted to be the one throwing it over the fence. It would have been a catastrophe if the big, sturdy Fisher-Price toy box landed squarely on the boy. Harriet's son succeeded. The plastic steering wheel toy landed with a thud on the patio, not on the little boy.

Harriet and her son bid the boy goodbye, his parents still nowhere in sight. But she was content as she had fulfilled her Easter checklist this year.

Mother and son made their way home.

Surprise, Surprise

"This was a bad idea," I mouthed over the speaker phone while cradling the wretched pot of cactus on my lap, as it swayed gingerly with every turn and bump on the road.

The day had started off like an anthology of mishaps. In case you hadn't noticed, these things tended to happen in the name of good intent.

Eugene and I go way back to junior school days in Indonesia. His mother had nearly named him Adonis. That name wouldn't have worked out. Let me tell you why.

Imagine an ass doctor called Adonis. His mother was really into Greek mythology when she was pregnant with him, and thought the name of a folkloric, handsome mortal apt for her new son. She neglected to consider that the mortal in the story was turned into a stag and got killed by an arrow. I guess she had not gotten to that part yet. She just liked the sound of it. Thankfully for my friend, his Mum finally opted for a safe choice, Eugene.

Eugene and I were destined to be friends. Luck had it that we kept bumping into each other in various countries throughout the remainder of our formal and tertiary education.

When we were 15 we were two school kids up to no good. Two decades later, apparently we were still up to no good. A flashback in time took me to a moment when Eugene and I pulled a prank on our classmate Evan's fried rice. The three of us were to meet in a coffee shop after school but Evan was late. His mountain of *nasi goreng* (fried rice) was waiting for him. It was too tempting. We thought it was a good idea to dig a discreet hole from the top of that fried rice a la a volcano, and stuff it with two types of very spicy chilli sauce, all unbeknownst to our friend. We giggled in the coffee shop's partitioned booth opposite Evan when he arrived and ate his food. Evan thought this was one hell of a strange fried rice, but he was famished and so he polished his plate. It resulted in lots of trips to the toilet later.

I eventually moved to Singapore for the rest of my high school education, and so did Eugene. When it came to Australia, on the first day of university orientation, guess who I bumped into.

Our final education meeting was as fellow postgraduate students in the UK, where my old friend, the class geek, triumphantly emerged as a haemorrhoid specialist. There is a proper name for doctors specialising in such a craft but as of now I can't recall what it is. Eugene was now the most popular, enterprising haemorrhoid doctor in town.

When I asked why he chose such a vocation, he said he was looking for something outside the box, that most people wouldn't do so there was less competition.

Laugh we might, but he made the right choice. He was now swimming in cash and you know what they say, 'Cash is King!' His day job of looking at his fellow mankind's *derrière* has proved financially fruitful. It is $500 per half an hour slot, $2,000 if he has to inject anything into said *derrière*. His usual opening line of, "It's not gonna hurt. If it hurts, then it means I poked at the wrong place," with an extra Ho Ho Ho added in for free, a line he trademarked. His practice at Mount Elizabeth Hospital is always overflowing with patients looking for some 'backdoor' relief.

That day happened to be a mutual friend's birthday. Gary lived in a government housing estate (Housing Development Board or HDB flat), in a suburb called Ang Mo Kio, 20 minutes from town. To be closer to his Mum, he said.

This was a good friend who had helped both of us a lot through the years, a bit like a big brother figure. He was turning 55. He had his flat all done up in a cool retro style (not our dad's kind of retro), and when one stepped past his door, it was like stepping into another world. He was perpetually single and enjoyed showing the ladies that other world past his door.

With all of these measures in place (mask, social distancing, only one person allowed to go out from each household and only for necessities or to feed the elderly), Eugene had been spinning his brain as to what would be a law abiding way to still celebrate with our friend.

For gifts, he came up with two items: a durian and a plant.

The durian is the spiky King of Fruits from Southeast Asia. Loved by most Asians, hated by Westerners. It is banned in many places and at best, regarded with suspicion. Westerners call it the 'blue cheese of fruits'.

I asked why this odd combination of pastoral choices. Eugene explained that Gary loved durians and he had mentioned about getting a plant for his flat.

I asked how exactly we were going to achieve this. He said we would each get one item, travel alone, and we would technically be feeding the 'elderly' (with durian and a plant). These were all legit activities, he argued.

"Fifty-five. Gary is ancient now, a senior citizen."

"Yeah, and we're middle-age."

If you see a tanned, fit, 'geriatric' in a Hawaiian shirt, that's Gary. He looks at least 10 years younger than his years and there is nothing old about him. A forever Peter Pan. I guess with the advent of Coronavirus, everyone else would be fully 'aged', aside from Gary.

Especially everyone doing bloody Home Based Learning.

Eugene said we were not socialising. We would just leave the items by his door. I thought yeah why not, a simple, drop off. He argued that, contactless it may be, but Gary would appreciate the personal touch.

So now, the big question was, who would get what. Divide and conquer, he said. At that, I quickly interjected,

"You get the durian."

"Why me?"

"Because you have a d*ck. And because I'm a soprano."

Reason did not have to be logical. I was, after all, a woman.

Also, sopranos were not supposed to do manual labour. We'd leave it to somebody else, as we were too busy preparing to die on stage most of the time. It took three hours for us to die on stage. It was hard work.

Quietly though I had foreseen that whoever was getting that durian was going to have to maybe open it, or smell like it, for the near future. I said I'd get the plant, from the supermarket next door. Because that was the only place that might have a plant for sale within this vicinity. I recalled they sold orchids.

Unfortunately though, the only plant the supermarket had on sale that I could get my hands on was a cactus. There were no dignified orchids or useful aloe vera, or anything else that day. Eugene said it was ok, just grab the cactus. Gary went to Mexico and loved it, so he must love cactus too, the wonder of his simple logic. After all a cactus requires the least maintenance.

Then I saw a priest who was a friend of my parents. I was not supposed to be out from the flat at all if it were up to them, the world was too dangerous right now. Oh no, he'd report me to my dad. I had forgotten I was wearing a mask (hence was not so easily recognised) and decided to make a run for it. When I realised I couldn't, I decided to counter-trail the old priest from aisle to aisle, every time moving further away, aiming for the cashier. I tripped while attempting a somersault to the cashier's counter, and although I did not land flat on my face, I was also trying to save the plant from getting crushed. I cut my fingers doing so. Fantastic. Such was my luck it happened to be the First-Aid aisle, band-aids were abound. Priest was none the wiser. Several leaps and bounds later, the wounded fugitive surreptitiously made it to the taxi stand.

In the meantime at Casa de Eugene. Eugene somehow managed to procure a durian. He thought he'd open it, don't make the birthday boy work on his special day. At least crack it open.

He discovered soon enough he may be adept with surgical tools for another kind of crack, but this was something beyond his realm. Eugene the sensitive new age guy tried the pincer, a hammer and a pair of pliers. He even considered throwing the bloody fruit on to the floor, before the hacksaw worked.

When it did, he touched base with me, to check which stage of the mission I had accomplished on my side.

We got into taxis, but things did not quite improve.

Mine went round and round as the driver was not too accustomed to the GPS. Eugene had initially arrived first, but, his taxi could only take cash payment which he had forgotten to bring. So off they went in search of an ATM, found one at an ESSO petrol station nearby. The first sight that confronted him inside that petrol station was a picture of his Ex, a former B-rated underwear model, on the cover of a women's magazine. She seemed to have a new set of bigger fake boobs than before, and she was not alone. Cozying up to her on that cover was a controversial new multimillionaire about town, an online sex-toy empire boss. Must be a lucrative business especially during these days that self-service was the norm. "I found love again!" was splashed in big bold red above their heads. Not Eugene's most auspicious day.

At Gary's housing complex. I saw Eugene from afar. He had turned up wearing all black, topped with black shades. He dressed like he was auditioning for *The Matrix*, so much for hiding in plain view. I did not approach but called his phone instead.

"I'm on stealth mode," he proudly said.

"It's mid-afternoon. Are you trying to attract attention? Like, you look obvious."

"It's not working out, is it?"

"No, it's not."

"Well, you look like it's Chinese New Year all over again."

In my bright red attire I suddenly spotted what I suspected was a Distancing Officer (not the police but one who could issue fines). Although we had not done anything wrong (yet), guilt was starting to seep in. Guilt, you see, was a powerful control tool of all the mothers of our previous generation.

Why oh why did I always get myself into this kind of sticky situation. Of all the stupid things we did before, I think this one took the cake. Decidedly. I was starting to kick myself mentally why did I let him convince me again. He told me to remain calm and saunter in with confidence, as if we lived there.

"If you get arrested just tell them you're a sovereign."

"Yeah that's so helped the crazy lady, I'm sure that'll help me too," I replied sarcastically.

Around that time there was a local incident of a major Covidiot who refused to wear a mask, and aggressively argued with officers saying she was a sovereign. She was charged in court.

We headed over nervously to the lifts, on opposite far ends of the block.

"No, we were not together. We came solo (no pun intended)," we'd rehearsed that line.

He would take Lift B, while I would take Lift A. We would arrive on the same floor. I discovered that the lifts on my side were under repair. Oh for goodness sake. I had to climb up. Gary had of course wanted to get lucky, hence, he chose level 8 for his flat. Eight stories to climb. Eight was supposed to be a lucky Chinese number. That sure didn't feel lucky to me.

On his side, Eugene and his half-opened durian was getting into the lift. He did not want to touch the lift buttons by hand and fumbled in his pocket for a pen or a key, and was trying to press the lift button using his shirt, as he forgot to bring a bottle of sanitiser. In the course of doing that, the spiky fruit fell on his foot. His operatic yelp accompanied by a litany of curses in various languages could be heard from my side of the block. Another casualty of the supposed birthday surprise.

We both finally reached level eight. When I fulfilled the Herculean task of reaching the eight floor on foot, I was huffing and panting, with the bloody cactus in tow. The weather was so hot my make-up had started to run.

During lockdown, the only make-up a lady needed was eye make-up which was precisely what I forgot. At least I had eyebrows on, or maybe half an eyebrow left at that stage. I could not help but notice that the cactus was not as erect as when I took it from the grocery store, just like my legs.

I saw Eugene limping from the opposite side. We both stopped on the spot and got on the phone again to reaffirm the next course of action.

He told me what happened to his foot. At that moment he suddenly realised I was wearing high heels. Men were good at parallel parking and ordinarily hunting wild beasts, but they do find recognising female accessories akin to rocket science.

"You climbed up wearing that? What were you thinking?"

"My boss told me a soprano is an instrument, and an instrument needs to look good."

Well I was an instrument with blisters on her feet. The price of beauty.

We were each six metres away from Gary's door.

"Eugene, I'm giving up," taking off my shoes. Cactus in right hand, shoes in left.

"I can't believe you're a quitter."

I whined that we should have done something completely mainstream. Like order delivery from a restaurant rescue group, my preferred form of altruism these days, or flowers, or an escort service, whichever might please him the most.

If this was not enough of a surprise, I was going to tell Eugene to perform a solo Hakka dance next. With Gary watching through the door several steps inside his flat. That should be amusing.

"Remind me again, why we're here?"

"We're here to save the downtrodden," Eugene replied patriotically, annoyingly so.

"From what, pray tell?" I hissed irritably into the phone, while looking around nervously.

"Boredom."

"Well it looks to me that right now we are the downtrodden," me gesturing to the miserable spiky plant and our battle injuries.

Our 12-metre apart phone *sotto-voce* argument carried on for an epic three minutes.

[Voices getting more and more distant as if carried by the wind].

Coda: one half-cracked durian and one semi-erect cactus stood happily ever after outside their new home.

21 Questions: Interview by the 'Porn Stars'

Whilst on lockdown, I had the good fortune of being interviewed by a group of 'Porn Stars'. It started off as a survey on social media. The question was, "If you could ask me one question right now, what would it be?"

Here were the ground rules.

- It should not be boring: nothing about food or mundane things.
- No questions on numbers: undergarment size, dimensions, weight or age.
- No names (especially those asking who I had dated of late),
- And questions that were too lewd in nature.
- Questions could be on any topic but preferably one surrounding the events of Coronavirus.

The audience participation was overwhelming. So many people asked their question and gave their secret porn star names.

Some were busy keying in their names on the 'porn star names generator' website, some consulted their partners, some supplied the name first and then the question later. Interesting how a lot of people were very forthcoming with supplying their desired porn star names. Maybe it was their hidden fantasy. Some questions were more serious in nature, while some were very cheeky.

Out of the hundred-odd questions submitted, 21 questions made the grade.

So these are my 21 Questions: Interview by the 'Porn Stars'. Them hurling questions one after another, and me trying to answer (or dodge) as best I could. Feel free to play your very own 21 questions, during your virtual catch-up with friends.

Enjoy!

RUSSO TORPEDO: What has Coronavirus made you realise in terms of your life?
A. That life is short. What (or who) we want to do or be, we better do it (or them) now.

FELICITY CHEONG: Do the men you date ask you to sing for your supper?
A. One or two did. Strangely they also offered me 'dessert'.

HUGH COCKMAN: Did you know that quarantine comes from the Italian word, *quaranta*? It was supposedly from the era of the Black Plague, when the Venetians demanded that all ships had to dock at the harbour for 40 days.

A. I didn't know, actually. That's very interesting (and ironic). Italians. 40 days at home. *Capisce*?

MR GOLDEN GUN: What has been your most awkward date?

A. With you. Actually come to think of it, with your best friend.

MISS PIGGY: Who's the first person (male, of course) you want to meet after Circuit Breaker ends.

A. My hairdresser.

LITTLE PASSION FRUIT: How do you juggle confinement with two young children, home schooling them with extra curricular activities, meals, food shopping, bonding with friends AND writing? How do you keep your sanity? Err, is that one question?

A. Ah. With pure magic and time travel. All from a bottle.

BONE DRY: What is the most important thing for you right now?

A. To not get COVID-19, and to suggest to the neighbour that the recorder is not a suitable instrument for their son.

PUSSY LOGAN: What was the worst thing you did when you were growing up that your parents didn't know about?

A. That the rat did not steal the little chicks in the night. It was I who accidentally left the cage door open. They shat all over my Dad's home office. He was not a happy camper.

CB BREAKER: What is your secret talent?

A. Sleep Walking.

T. LEX: If you had a chance to be anyone else for a day (without any responsibilities or liabilities), who would it be?

A. Me, just without any responsibilities or liabilities.

PINKY PANTHER: If you were given a new life, what would you be?

A. A man. They don't have periods.

DICK NASTY: Can you imagine being in quarantine with me, just the two of us?

A. Yes. And the double homicide after.

SURF ME: Do you like bondage?

A. Do you?

DARLENE CREAM PUFF: How many men dropped by your home to stick their neck out for you in this quarantine?

A. I lost count. OK, I lied. Four Romeos. One tried projecting his voice, i.e. shouting, from downstairs to my not very high windows, the rest were slightly more rational. They arranged third-party deliveries.

JASON FULLER: Is the lockdown likely to make you indulge in voyeuristic or exhibitionistic tendencies?

A. Positively voyeuristic. Covidiot sightings from my windows.

DICK FALCON: If you were to make a special Circuit Breaker Cocktail, what would you put in it?

A. Sleeping potion. We will all be Sleeping Beauty and wake up only when this nightmare is over.

RAM-ME: If you could wish something upon your worst Ex, what would it be?

A. That he finally realises his dream to be an astronaut and flies to the moon. He can stay there for a while.

PIERRE JAXEM: Have your goals changed during this COVID-19 period?

A. A dose of an intellectual question for us all. Well this book we are reading was written during lockdown. So that's one. Other than remaining alive even if life sucks. It's preferable to be alive then dead—perhaps just surviving. Taking stock. Slow down. And really making the best use of our time, at this time. It's perhaps a God-given opportunity to execute our delayed projects, reconnect with loved ones at home, or learn new skills. Like opening a yoghurt tub with one hand [SLURP].

JACK THE PIMP: How many proposals have you had from younger men to be your toy boy and you their sugar momma?

A. One, if you count yourself.

MISTRESS SISSI: If you could have dinner with anyone in the world, dead or alive, who would it be?

A. Mr Bean. He would have a good solution and we don't have to swallow Clorox.

EDWIN ORLANDO DORIAN CRUZ: What are the things that you used to like in the last decade that you don't like anymore?

A. Cotton candies, battery-operated devices and mother-in-laws, in no particular order.

And finally, the million-dollar bonus question! [DRUM ROLL]

MILLION DOLLAR BABE: Who was the best sex of your life?

A. The best is yet to come.

* * *

[Typing own name on the 'Porn Star Name Generator']

Love Thy Neighbour

"One hundred and one, one hundred and two." I was not counting sheep. It was in fact the following day whilst on my Covidiot sightings by the window that I caught sight of my neighbour slash best-friend of too many years, Allen.

He was with the throng of other non-social distancing Covidiots by the river. Probably running his usual errands at the mall.

Allen was the previously mentioned messenger of bad news who informed me of the confirmed COVID-19 case in our condo.

Our interesting friendship (once considered unlikely), had started when he dated a close female friend of mine. He was young, eligible and buffed, with his trademark firm handshake. Outings of three (of us) marked their brief relationship.

It soon became apparent to me, the default observer, they were two very good people that were just not meant to be together. I found myself admiring wallpapers of Japanese restaurants while frosty verbal darts were exchanged over my head. The relationship ended in an anti-climax with two parallel lines of irate text messages coming in from both of them on their disastrous trip to Paris.

I had kept my peace. They bumped into each other from time to time at my events (if not at the Jelita branch of Cold Storage supermarket), and were civil for my sake.

She proceeded to marry a gregarious European and together they contributed annually to Singapore's population. These happy accidents happened whilst on annual holiday at the mountainous hometown of said European. One after the other. They have four, going on to number five now. Maybe it was the air. The Singapore government has commended their efforts as a model couple.

Our friendship has outlived their relationship and my horrendous marriage. Through sheer coincidence, Allen had also become my neighbour.

Allen was kind but eccentric. His military precision with regards to time stressed the shit out of me. Let's just say my sense of timing was rather elastic. You see whenever we had an appointment he'd text me with minute-by-minute notice reminders:

- Will pick you up at 7.32pm;
- 7 minutes away;
- 5 minutes away;
- Approaching your lobby.

While he was going through this exercise I would be drying my dripping hair frantically. All this while muttering to myself, this was the reason why he was still single.

Allen's one redeeming quality was of course his unmatched generosity. He was very charitable, especially to people dear to him. Among the neighbourhood groups he had also endeared himself to my other friends, Heather and Steve, who also live in the vicinity. Imagine the sitcom *Friends*, minus the inbreeding (unless for those already married).

While I was on the verge of being a newborn Covidol, Allen was still firmly in the Covidiots camp. No mask (who needed a mask anyway), still going around everywhere on his endless string of dates. We got daily photo updates as to his dates' food, hands and busts. But never the face. He was quite discreet in his own way. The neighbours and I were worried of catching the virus from him, you know even when one was not showing any symptoms he or she could be a carrier. But we dared not protest, very Asian.

What was most bizarre was that Allen had been in his usual generous form, giving out masks and sanitisers to others, whose value were by then akin to gold, whilst for himself he did not wear any. We fretted in silence but one fine day the neighbourhood jointly decided to influence him as best we could to please take precautions and wear all these items as a Covidol would.

Now, for sure this COVID-19 pandemic was going to affect friendships further. We did not want to offend our dear friend, but we were also scared shitless if not for his and our sakes then for our more vulnerable family members.

How to go about this, we thought. Ah, let's avoid. So no-one would be upset or hurt.

Once, Allen was at the mall on his usual errands or food purchases. Heather and I happened to be on our anxious quick errands, separately. Each was armed with masks and sanitisers. PING. A message on the group chat.

"Hello! Are you two ladies here? I will pass you some stuff!"

(He was our neighbourhood Santa Claus and was always shopping for loved ones).

We did not know what to say. We had always hung out together. How now?

The two of us ladies were at opposite corners of the same floor, and he was on another floor. Suddenly we spotted him and his shopping bags, from the middle of the atrium, on the floor just below.

"Ahhhh..! OMG. He's there!"

"Oh shit, shit, shit... Where?"

"In front of the lingerie shop, one floor down. Look left."

"What's he doing in front of the bra shop?"

"How would I know? Hide. Hide. Let's hide."

"Let's say we're at home."

"What if he sees us?"

"Cover your face. Use your bag or hat."

I don't see you, you don't see me. It seemed that I had not progressed much since kindergarten. But, when panic sets in, often we become our original, delusional selves.

Heather, in her wide-brimmed hat, was carrying way too many shopping bags herself and hence a little too visible. Whilst trying to make for the exit, Allen spotted her, "Hey! I saw you!! Hullo! Look down!"

Heather froze, turned around and gave an awkward obligatory wave. That was it. One down.

I made two large hops to hide behind a gigantic flower pot nearby. Never had I been so grateful to be vertically challenged as I was then.

Each to her own now. And running home with hands flapping in the wind I did.

Short Circuited

Just the other week, more shit hit the fan and we discovered hundreds more confirmed COVID-19 cases in Singapore. The Circuit Breaker was announced. No, it was not a lockdown, just more and more measures were announced daily.

First, all offices were to close and we all had to Work From Home (WFH). I'd address this in the following chapters. Then schools followed and the children had to have Home-Based Learning (HBL).

The following days, we were drip-fed the actual extent of the measures.

No home or social gatherings. We couldn't see people who did not live under the same roof as us. Final icing on the cake: no more dropping kids at the grandparents. Under pain of a maximum penalty of a $1,000 fine or a jail term. Singapore is a Fine City, it worked. Watch and learn. There will be drones and police enforcing strict order, as expected.

The first people who freaked out about this were my neighbours and I, being a very close-knit group. More parallel, bilateral and group messages lamented these newest measures.

"Oh no. How? I don't see you for a month?"

"Don't be paranoid. I'll check with my lawyer. Let's see what the Bill wording actually says."

"I'm sure if it's only two or three of us it should be ok."

No, it was not ok. The whole Red Dot was trying our best on a grassroots level to help curb the spread of this wretched virus. The longer we did not cooperate, the longer we would be short circuited.

I guess any bad news takes time to seep in.

There was a loophole however: we could still go to a park to exercise. Wicked gnomes we were, we each quickly came out with a solution on how to continue to see each other whilst still complying with the rules.

I proposed as such, "Say, if by coincidence, some pure coincidence of course, I happen to chance upon you at say the Botanical

Gardens tomorrow at 5pm at the Swan Lake and we maintain a 2-metre distance each and sit on different benches? That is going to work, no? We can speak on the phone and just stare at each other."

"We don't go in the same car?"

"We go separately."

"One of us had better be running, on the spot, at least. They said exercise."

"We can take turns, or we'll just let Allen and Steve run around the pond while we sit."

So there we were, all four of us. Separate individual arrivals, armed with masks and a water bottle each whose content you could perhaps guess was not mainly H2O. We stuck our necks around like penguins in the park with walkie-talkies, pretending we didn't know each other.

I saw a woman pointing from afar.

"Is that you? We look ridiculous." Laugh.

"Ho ho ho ho. Yes, it's me."

"That's Allen, he's brought his whole cupboard, hasn't he?? LOL. Bla bla bla.."

Wave to the right, wave to the left.

We spaced out at equal safe distances around the big pond and went on conference WhatsApp call, giggling all the way. How wonderful. Love thy neighbours.

Then I woke up.

On Resilient Business Models

The one big question looming on every single woman's mind on the topic of dating prospects was, "Is he The One?"

In my humble opinion, we have all came across The One at some point of time, just not necessarily The Correct One. For example I've met The One, The Wrong One.

In the quest of searching for The One during lockdown, three ladies fancied they might have found a possible solution to narrow down the unknown, while discussing all things spiritual and not so spiritual.

As one might have observed, there were some forms of businesses that did well during the time of the pandemic. One unexpected business that flourished during the lockdown period of COVID-19 (other than Netflix and the ever resilient porn industry) was the field of fortune telling, or astrology (or professional charlatan, quoting my friend, a police officer in-charge of frauds).

Enter, the clairvoyant.

"I went to see a clairvoyant the other day. Online, of course."

"What would you like to know?"

"Well, when would this pandemic end, among others. And where was my new boyfriend? Last time he told me I would meet someone soon."

"I would have asked for the lotto number," said I, *The Merry Widow*.

One of us in the group had remained strangely silent, observing the conversation.

During this period, people were out of jobs and people were stuck at home. Some people were happier than others. Most people wanted hope, and to cling on to some kind of certainty (or the illusion of it) out of our collectively bleak future. We all wanted to know what was going to happen, if and when, we all came out of this.

Fortune-telling has one rather large customer base, single women. If men were into porn, women were into horoscopes and dating advice. All these factors put together made a perfect setting for the psychic industry.

Single people were looking to be not so single anymore. It sucked drinking alone at home during lockdown, you could never finish a bottle. Tell me about it. Women who were married were starting to put out banners that said 'Free Husband Available'.

See, there is still hope for singles. Some people's trash may be somebody else's treasure! Take it from me, I just picked something off the recycling bin this afternoon that the neighbours threw away and made it mine. Glass jars and cartons for kids' art projects. Not exactly comparable with the descendants of Adam (who ate the forbidden fruit) but you get my drift.

Fortune-telling can be done online. Payment is also online. No need to arrange for delivery. It appeals to both spirituality and superstition. It has been so for hundreds of years. It is an old profession, arguably as old as porn. Some clairvoyants are more famous than others. Some have even achieved global fame. They are known for their high emotional intelligence, perception and insights. They are charismatic. A lot of their advice is really humane. It tugs at your heartstrings. Their success depends on how good is their ability to know exactly what to say to people who are in distress. A soothing presence, so to speak.

And then, a few days later.

Brenda, my lawyer friend, was an unlikely customer. After that conversation we girlfriends had, she quietly private messaged our other friend for the contact details of the fortune-teller she was raving about. Brenda suddenly remembered there was something unsettled in her life that she would like an answer for.

Dialling the given number, my lawyer friend had only one question.

To The One.

………………………………..

…………………………….

…………………………….

(who got away).

The Onion Challenge

"You look ridiculous," is my typical non-starter mumble to my friend Margaret, every time we have to line-up in a row to take a group photo with our girls. Nobody wants to stand next to Margaret for these photo ops. All seven ladies would be elbowing each other not to be next to her in the photo. Not because she has an infectious disease, but it is because she looks so ridiculously fit and toned that next to her, we can't help but feel slightly less than fabulous.

Margaret, named after Britain's Iron Lady Margaret Thatcher, is one of the few women who had done the Iron Man Challenge, three times. Imagine Linda Hamilton in the *Terminator* minus the crazy hair. She is a wellness guru plus public relations extraordinaire whose idea of relaxing is doing five classes of pilates and yoga on a

Saturday. If Margaret had to name one of her superpowers, in my opinion it would be 'dragging a truck tyre with bare hands'. Once one of the guys in our group had to choose between escorting three of us ladies to a certain parking lot, or Margaret alone, to a different parking lot, late at night after a group drinking session. He chose to escort the tree hapless flabby ladies to the parking lot instead of Margaret. Margaret could take care of things. He said in fact it might be in the would-be-perpetrator's best interest not to provoke Margaret in any terrain, as she also found hand-to-hand combat (i.e. slapping sleazy men) relaxing.

Such a perfect person must have a flaw, one might think. Her little nephew thought so too. When she was babysitting him, Margaret tried telling him to go to sleep, but instead he threw a royal tantrum. The little man told my female warrior friend, "You're not a very nice lady," but I beg to differ. She's one of the nicest, gentlest people I know, although in her nephew's defence I've never been told to sit in a corner by Margaret. Or else.

In this mass quarantine period, different people do different things to occupy their time at home. Some take to painting and many free people bake. A highly-creative individual (a borderline nutcase) took to stealing female neighbours' undergarments. He had a prized collection of 25 bras and panties when the authorities got to him. *Veni, vidi, vici,* only in this case slightly adapted to the modern context: I come, I see, I steal. See how judgemental we are, for all we know the man might be just looking for materials to make homemade masks with. With the global mask shortage, a bra makes a logical replacement.

In Margaret's case, she is a pescatarian (i.e. she eats leaves and steamed fish), so no baking there.

Her idea of creativity instead translates to doing indoor physical challenges such as The Hand Stand T-Shirt Challenge, popularised by Hollywood celebrities Tom Holland, Jake Gyllenhaal and Ryan Reynolds. Margaret filmed herself doing it with her eyes closed. It was too easy. She bested our male friends in the challenge. The brave troopers, not only T-Shirts were not successfully applied, but one unfortunately suffered a loss of shorts too in the midst of a Facebook Live filming (it was a loose, airy basketball shorts). His upside down bum on air for all to see. It certainly managed to attract attention online. It's ok, I consoled my friend. Bad publicity is still publicity.

Margaret can be relied upon to come out on top. For her pre-wedding photo shoot last year she flawlessly executed a variety of handstand yoga poses, with her now husband pictured lying in a *Shavasana* position in virtually all of the frames (i.e. resting pose, lying down flat on your back) with her floating vertically on top, kissing him. It was an incredible stance I could totally achieve. I could pull it off. I could do his pose.

See, a rabbit jumps around and moves quickly, but it lives only for eight years, whereas a turtle barely moves, and looks lazy, but it can live up to 150 years. From this instance I deduce that the secret to longevity (in contrary to popular belief) is to be a turtle.

For her next challenge Margaret started a trend of balancing an onion while doing modified push-ups or yoga poses, with an aim to move the onion to and fro on your back without it slipping onto the floor. I challenged her to incorporate her husband into her new challenge for couples, maybe to safeguard the onion. See if this particular challenge will further place our male friends in a pickle.

While I was observing Margaret and her onion achieve the impossible, I got to think about life deeply. My earlier New Year Resolution (other than going to a mountain to avoid straight men, as they have proven to be quite a source of headaches for me personally) was to be fitter and to lose a bit of weight.

But then 2020 being a rather unpredictable year, my Withings digital scale suddenly classified my BMI and body fat content as unknown, where before it could immediately detect the weight patterns of the usual suspects standing on the scale.

In the meantime I've got my own personal challenge on how to make my favourite bowl of instant noodles disappear in five minutes. Let me work on that while I figure out how best to imitate Margaret and her floating (now viral) onion very carefully, for the next month or so.

Please do not try this at home. I'm a professional.

On Weird Dietary Options

Darwin said our ancestors were monkeys, though perhaps slightly more eloquently put. I'm a singer not a bard, and with teaching the kids eight hours a day, I've got literally half a brain cell left at the end of each day.

My dad vehemently argued against this, perhaps a little too defensively so, for one whose forefathers were clearly humans. Although in the case of certain individuals (yes, guess who, don't sue), their behaviour did resemble the said ancestral apes, as their evolution in terms of common sense and human decency seemed to be stuck in that stage of evolution.

My point is, the species that adapts, survives.

With the supermarket shelves bare, I have not been able to buy

Leggo brand bolognese sauce anywhere, despite trekking high and low on foot (meaning to the two neighbouring shopping malls to my right and to my left of my home) and of course on the internet. I was also perpetually on the lookout for my particular type of *Indomie Soto*. It too suddenly seemed to have followed the Dodo bird and was extinct. For me it had taken the crown from *Indomie Goreng Sate*, the glorious comfort food of my university days. Maybe taste palates change with age. Yes, go figure. I have an Indonesian villager's palate. Simple taste, simple life. As I always say, it goes in the same way, and it goes out the same other way. I am an avid consumer of vintage Bordeaux so my friend Jonathan had called me out on that. Well, maybe one or two sinful delights. Life is short.

Imagine if the elephants were presented with a mouse to eat, or, the tigers were forced to go vegan. I would wholly empathise with those tigers deeply, as the only circumstances where I would go vegan were to be the actual apocalypse, not this one just yet, but literally.

We were all taught that humans were omnivores (i.e. eat any food that move or doesn't move), or so my Biology teacher said. But I pretty much slept throughout that subject and very unfortunately for me, only woke up just in time to do a practical test, on skeletons. The legend in my school was that it was a real human skeleton. Not wanting to repeat that test, I aced the skeleton part but I failed the rest of the Biology topics. How's that for motivation.

Seemed to me though that we were not so omnivorous anymore. There were the vegans, and then the vegetarians (until now, I still can't tell the difference, I just know they are the hardest tribe to go for dinner with. I know, I dated one. What a pain). And then there were those for religious reasons, Halal, Kosher (same but not same, funny that they hated each other eh), and then those who did not eat *wagyu* beef, Buddhists, I believe?

Suffice to say that the panic buying of late had resulted not just in the craze for toilet paper, but in off food choices for people with differing dietary requirements.

What if people who did not like spicy Asian food, had only chilli laden options, or, if vegans were left with only meat?

I wonder what would they choose, the high holy way, or survival.

As if to answer my question, on my next trip to the supermarket (of course, the government subsidised supermarkets) I was confronted with the sight of a well-built Caucasian man of indefinite origin contemplating a row of canned food. These days they seemed to be flocking on my humble supermarket. I guess they realised they were being ripped off by the expat supermarkets. I saw that he was considering the spicy Ayam brand tuna that was my staple food in college. He had a singular choice. There were no other flavours, nor a single can of corned beef or luncheon meat left. He grabbed six cans of these. I wonder how he went at home with those. I assumed that Caucasians do not take spicy food, but maybe I was wrong.

On that note a friend of mine told me of this Singapore-brand luncheon meat that was truly Singapore, but Made in China. It had a Singapore icon on the packaging and the tin said that it was born in Singapore. Hmmmm. It was all about perspectives you see. *When you believe* by Whitney Houston and Mariah Carey is an appropriate accompanying soundtrack for this 'Singapore' luncheon meat anecdote.

These days I'd always seemed to assign karaoke soundtracks for differing odd scenes. Somehow it gave some kind of comic effect to unfortunate happenings. Convenient when one had her bluetooth earphones plugged in her ears when going out and about, solo, obviously. It was a perfect cover when eavesdropping on people's conversations as a writer.

Vegans having to eat meat, their hymn be, Celine Dion's *Think Twice*, or the ever depressing *End of the World* by Skeeter Davis.

Muslims confronted with non-halal food, or Buddhists left with no options but beef, *No, no, no* by Destiny's Child and Wyclef Jean.

Pescatarians were the fishy vegan bunch, normally by choice. These days with the fish shortage, their national anthem could be *Vegetable Song* by The Singing Walrus.

Now, the gluten-free group! I genuinely felt for this group as it was normally medically required, a necessity, not a lifestyle choice. It was hard enough finding normal food products let alone gluten-free ones during the pandemic period. I'd say, Freddy Mercury's *I Want to Break Free* would do them justice. Just the other day my dear friend Steph had to drive to five supermarkets in search of gluten-free pasta, and still had no luck.

Non-dairy, lactose intolerant. Supermarkets stripped-bare of dairy alternatives? Must be those vegetable people hoarding them. If they must, they must. They'll just have to gas their way through the night, and pretty much the whole lockdown. Recommended to sleep alone. Perfect for current distancing requirements. Their accompanying soundtrack? *Gas, Gas, Gas* by Manuel.

Finally, taking our hats off for those with allergies, say shellfish allergies. When it was life threatening then one had no choice but to abide.

But if it was a mild case: a diplomat friend of mine always specified his dietary requirement as no crustacean. However he was a foodie, and only had a mild case of skin rash when exposed to the substance. Often, if the crab or lobster was tantalising enough, my friend would gladly suffer the consequences and look the other way in favour of food orgasm, even if it meant he would resemble the colour of his food by the end of the evening. Serenaded by Connie Francis, his anthem be, *I'll Close My Eyes*.

Meanwhile closer to home, a certain family member (no, not my mum) who refused to be named is absolutely anal about food. She would find very specific origins for each food produce all over the city-state. Of late she had also gone organic. Yes some people do like to make life more difficult than it was for themselves. There was some logic to it though. She does not buy China produce, "They can fake everything! Scared, lah. Not because I so *atas* (i.e. high-class) but scared of China things. Even eggs they can fake!" Fair enough.

Another requirement, no Japanese produce or seafood. Radiation, she claimed sombrely, even though I gently reminded her that it was just one city affected. No dubious South American frozen meat for her too.

Garlic in particular, must be French. Don't ask me why. While Australia and Malaysia were her desired destinations, not for resorts, but for vegetables.

Do you wonder if she finally adapted?

[John Mayer singing *Waiting On The World To Change* in the background, while I chomp on my newly procured premium grade Ma Ling, China's famed pork luncheon meat at home. The best and obtained from the expat's supermarket]

* * *

> "It is not the strongest of the species that survives,
> nor the most intelligent that survives.
> It is the one that is most adaptable to change."
> — Charles Darwin (1809–1882).

Under One Roof

"Check this out man. He is a P I M P! Alright, this is how I should roll…" said my childhood friend Jin. This was a call from the US that came in at 2am Singapore time.

So within this period he got wind of the news that a certain Royal had decided to put himself in a self-imposed isolation in a luxury hotel with no less than 20 women. This was news that excited Jin as well as many other males. What a fantasy. Getting locked up with 20 beautiful females who attended to your every whim.

The news channels had not been able to ascertain if his existing four wives and concubines were amongst the aforementioned ladies or not. Jin had sorely complained with regards to the number.

"Well we are not sure if it was indeed 20 or a more conservative number, like, two," I theorised with my eyes shut.

Jin was adamantly still on point, "That's beside the point, I mean who does 20 ladies a night?"

"What is your problem? LOL. Let's not begrudge him. If he can, he can. Why not. After all if we were a billionaire Royal we might just do the same. Heck, make it 40, why stop at 20," came my nonchalant reply while I started daydreaming what kind of harem I would compile. Hey, I'm all for emancipation.

Jin concluded, "They have a roster. They MUST have a roster. I mean who does 20 women a night?"

I replied that then again it might just be the news outlets looking for juicy materials out of desperation. Any other news better than the gloom and doom we have had to face of late. The ladies could have been his mother and his aunts? No? I could feel his eyes rolling.

Ok maybe not.

According to Jin's theory and he had many theories. We've been friends ever since we were six. One of his many infamous theories was that chickens cannot swim, erroneously applied while we were in my parents' backyard plastic paddling pool. He had not taken into account that the water was only about 15 cm deep and that the chicken was mightily pissed off. Jin had taken her eggs without permission and unfortunately had been seen by her. She had chased him all around the makeshift pond for revenge. Few people other than Jin could attest how it felt being slapped by a chicken. And hence my obsession with live chickens too.

Sorry to digress. Coming back to the point. Yes, it's 2am and I told him to leave me alone but he would not stop ranting. It was cheaper to talk to me than a shrink, he said.

Jin continued. These wives and (more) wives had a three-prong approach as to their career progression: first as a flight attendant, re-emerging as generals, and next, as wife. Unconventional, but it worked. Look, I'm not judgemental. Few people would be judgemental when they were half asleep.

I flatly thanked him and conveyed that I had no desire to be a general or a concubine at the moment and hoped he could come to terms to not being locked up with 20 women.

I guess some people got to choose who they go on lockdown with. Most of us don't. But then again, most of us do not have concubines.

As for me, while in lockdown, I had the default choice of:
me, myself, and I;
my domestic helper,
underaged children,
Tommy and Flynn.

Sorry to burst your fantasy bubble but Tommy and Flynn were no Chris Hemsworth/Daniel Henney lookalikes. They were our family pet hamsters.

It is interesting how these glorified rodents behave remarkably like humans. Tommy and Flynn are brothers. They came from the same litter. When they started off (we bought them at a few weeks old), they were exactly the same size but with entirely different behaviour. Tommy was the athletic sort while Flynn was the fat one.

Tommy would eat mindfully, with good manners, outside the food container. Meanwhile, Flynn would hop onto the food container, forcing his brother to eat around him, or in most instances his brother would end up eating later.

Tommy exercised, doing regular, faithful runs on the hamsters wheel. When Flynn tried to exercise, I could hear him from another room as he had grown rather fat, and it normally did not last a few seconds until he dropped flat on the wheel and gave up exercising altogether. Sounded eerily familiar.

Well my friend Alvin had wisely summed up, in the absence of pleasurable pursuits derived from women and outside experiences, he would do just the same as the hamsters: Eat. That would be the only pleasure left in life.

On another note, my luck with men has not been so stellar of late. Be they related to me by birth or not, and of dimensions tall or short, I found them all a headache last year.

These were their general categories and the problems they caused.
- Man who made me = different opinions problem.
- Man of horrid, nightmarish past = legal and mental health problems.

- Man who was my neighbour = social problem.
- Man of present/future/no future = just simply, problem.
- Man who fixed my appliances (but always destroyed something else in the midst of doing it) = household problem.

Seemed to me that: MEN = PROBLEM.

Conclusion: Avoid all (straight) men.

Options:
A. Go to a mountain somewhere and swear off men for good.
B. Stick to women and gay friends from now on.
C. All of the above.

This subjective conclusion elicited protests from all sorts of factions, mainly close male friends of course. So to be fair, within this period of seclusion other than binge watching men in skirts on Netflix (two dimensional figures never hurt), I thought a far more productive use of my time was to conduct a comparative study between hamsters and men, seeing the only males I happened to cohabitate with currently are these two hamsters, and see which breed was better for my mental health.

A few considerations came to mind. I had heard that the better looking they are, the worse their attitude. For example the snow white crystal type is very pretty but it bites and is known to be bad tempered. Apparently hamsters are like humans. We were advised to get the same gender and males.

Females have bouts of PMS, and a couple would sire plenty of little hamsters in no time. They would hump, and I did not wish to wake up to a hamster farm in my little flat.

So we got ourselves the grey striped sapphires. They were ranked third in terms of good looks and therefore less aggressive. They were good for kids to keep as pets.

These are the findings of the study:

"HAMSTERS VS HUMANS"
A Comparative Study

Data drawn from over a week of cohabiting in the same home with a pair of male hamsters and drawing from past sample space with male humans. Note: inclusive of all males, not just various types of partners but relatives and housemates as well.

MALE HAMSTERS
- Feed it
- Fill and replace water container
- Clean up after their shit (literally)
- Physical contact: Pat it, coo to it (I sing to it too and they start to recognise their mama now)
- Bath: Give bath weekly
- Relatives & Friends: N/A.
- Give the creature some space (lest you get bitten)
- Appreciation: be glad for every day that the creature remains alive and moving.
- Noise level: cute and tolerable.

MALE HUMANS

- Feed him
- Water: he could trot to the kitchen and take it himself.
- Clean up after his shit (Figurative, as in clutter).
- Physical contact: Have sex with him, often. (Not advisable for relatives although housemates might be a possibility).
- Bath: encourage him to shower twice a day, especially when you live near the equator.
- Tell him how magnificent he was in various things he held dear and what a unique stud he was in bed (be it true or not).
- Relatives and friends: Be nice to his relatives and friends. Especially his mother.
- Do not correct/direct him if he is driving and lost, just say what a lovely wonderful evening drive you have (even though it was in circles).
- Give the creature some space (lest you get bitten too, one way or the other).
- Appreciation: be gracious with any kind of effort or little kind gestures he's made, also of gifts (even if he has given you a vacuum cleaner two years in a row).
- Also be glad for everyday that he remains alive and moving (especially if his hobby is extreme sports).
- Noise level: depends on said hobby, and at night, just accept.

Conclusion:

Eh... Your verdict?

The (Not-So) Secret Garden

It was once again the Universe versus Ben.

After that episode of his missing pants during the video conference call with his lady boss and colleagues, he thought the best course of action was to go for his annual run. These days we were all runners, whether or not we had previously been one, anything to get out of the house. Right, East Coast Park. But no, the beaches were closed.

Before he left for the park my friend consulted me on the proper decorum of frequenting a park. I said, first things first, mask, for sure.

"Mask, eh. Yeah I got it, somewhere. From the community centre, right? But I don't know where it is now."

"You know those YouTube masks made out of bras? Just in case you got one lying around you could cut it in half and use," I suggested not very usefully. The alternative was those masks sold online specifically for fanatic runners which look like the face guard of Batman's enemy, you know, Tom Hardy's character in the movie *The Dark Knight Rises*.

"Goodness, I will do no such thing."

Of course.

Ben informed me that someone had mailed him a book on jogging. It was inspiring. I asked how bored one had to be to read a book on jogging? Surely we all knew how to jog?

Anyway seeing as the babes by the pool had not made an appearance in a month, and that he was newly single, Ben decided to go to a park. You know, his annual run, he said. After all they said exercise made people happy. Happiness was all the rage these days, with everyone on house arrest. At that stage we were allowed to hop around happily in the park so long as we maintained a minimum one-metre distance from one another and only went with people of the same household.

Ben deliberated carefully and chose the Botanical Gardens. At that stage we all had become park conservators too, and we could check crowd traffic on the NPark website. The website indicated a low crowd. Very good.

His control freak inner voice thought best to arrive prepared. He had heard all about it, and worked out a set of general rules for himself before departing for a park during this time of social distancing.

- "To avoid head-on collision with anybody heading your way: jump as far as you can. Jump to the right, jump to the left, doesn't matter. So long as you maintain distance from him." He wrote him specifically.
- "When encountering a runner: Hold your breath!! The droplets from the sweat reachs 10 metres. Or else seek alternative path."
- "Spotted an Ex? Turn 180 degrees around and walk the other way. If all else fails, cover your face."
- "If you see people you know, pretend you don't know them or else both will be Fined."
- "Further notes for friends, if you see your mother-in-law, make a run for it."

Best to abide by the rules, as Singapore is a fine city, and the lawmakers have taken it up a notch, $300 for the first offence and $1,000 for the subsequent one. Even going out with your own girlfriend in public would be one hell of an expensive date.

But Ben was not going with a date. He reckoned if the hot babes by the pool were not going to make an appearance, then he was going to find them, at the park.

He managed to locate his work-out gear. Oh, a little too tight. Maybe the dryer shrank it. But it still fit.

Upon his arrival, he was greeted by the sight of two identically-dressed young men being whisked away by officers. They were both clearly not observing the social distancing rule and on top of that, were not wearing masks. And low crowd, it said? Seemed to Ben that every Tom, Dick and Harry, and their dogs were at the Botanical Gardens. How was he going to keep a perpetual 1-metre distance from all those rapidly moving targets?

He observed all the seats in the park had these Xs marked on alternative seats. Big, and not the kind of Xs he liked.

Not five minutes in and already he had to dodge four joggers. It was like a game of PacMan. Further, Ben had read somewhere (must have been the jogging manual), that the perspiration of these joggers could still be traced in the air four to ten metres behind them, along with the Coronavirus, had they been silent carriers of the deadly virus. Not sexy. One coming up! Swerve to the left. He nearly fell into a bush trying to dodge the man.

He carried on jogging, and spotted some attractive ladies in scanty workout gear by the swan pond. Ah, the view when one enjoyed nature. Ben's mood suddenly improved tremendously.

At that moment, he could sense a runner right behind him, that huffing and panting sound and the heavy pounding of steps. Ben ran faster. But alas! Dead right ahead was his Ex! And to his horror, she was with her mother. Remain calm, he told himself. She hadn't spotted you. He took a decisive, wobbly 180 degree U-Turn, steadfastly sticking to his set of rules he prepared earlier. Back on safe zone. He pressed on, as quickly as he could. Turned around and glanced once. Ah, to his relief, his Ex and her dragon of a mother were no longer in view.

Soon he got distracted by more attractive looking ladies in midriff-baring tight lycra gear. He thought, why not live life in the fast lane. Nothing to lose, treat it like a masked ball in the park (except it was surgical masks, not Venetians). Oh you wretched Coronavirus, you're cramping my style, he lamented inwardly. But he was going to give it his best. He gave a suggestive nod and a wink towards the ladies, announcing his glorious presence. Thanks to the virus, tomorrow may never come so there was no time for inane posturing when it came to mating (or any possibility of it).

One accidental turn of the head, at the 11 o'clock direction, clearly seen ahead, were his Ex and her mother. They had somehow teleported themselves, at a very unsafe five-metre distance away, heading towards the taxi stand at the Tanglin Gate.

Two steps right ahead of him, a massive red jungle fowl suddenly reared its petrifying face. Ben and roosters had never been friends. Be it during his stint in the army or throughout his childhood.

A stumble and a splash later in a bid to avoid both his Ex and the rooster, Ben found himself in the shallow koi pond. Lucky for him it was only knee deep and not the oceanic swan pond or the murky turtle pond at the other parts of the Botanical Gardens, I remarked later when told of his misadventure. The ladies in their workout gear certainly took notice, but most of all, the two ladies he was so keen to avoid.

Confronted by the sight of her lovely ankles as she stood peering above him on the wooden path, as he was about to heave himself up with as much dignity as he could muster, Ben heard that familiar British accent, "Hello, fancy meeting you here."

It was certainly a jog to remember.

The New Normal

The Coronavirus altered many aspects of life, undoubtedly creating many new trends and hobbies.

All of us have had to adapt.

What follows is a mini glossary of these new habits, with some (hopefully) helpful explanations on the topic. For readers of the current time, these are some useful precautionary suggestions. For readers of the future, this was how things were at that time.

NEW TRENDS:
Wearing Masks. It was a new normal. Top of the list. Would cost you $300 not to. Face shield also recommended.

Washing hands while singing the whole Happy Birthday song (or anything lasting 20 seconds or more).

Sanitising hands. Every time we touch anything in public transport, say when taking a cab, after putting on the seatbelt and upon closing the door of said cab.

Grocery Shopping:
Sanitising if one must do grocery shopping in person. Every time one touched an object (in my case, until it actually became dangerously slippery).

When taking possession of a grocery trolley, wipe the handles and baskets with disinfecting wipes.

Upon reaching home, wash hands, remove all clothes (even if you've only worn them for an hour), and wipe all door handles and light switches with disinfectant.

Grocery delivery. Staying up until 3am for supermarkets' new delivery slots to be released and then giving out a shoutout to other desperate individuals. By the way, get used to broken eggs if you're having them delivered.

The groceries themselves. Upon them reaching home, wipe each item with disinfecting wipes as was told that the virus can survive on different substances for up to five days.

Toilet paper rationing was the natural progression.

HBL. The wretched, torturous Home Based Learning occupied most daytime activities and colonised the dining table. And stemming from HBL was the trend of day drinking parents (i.e. daydrinkers).

WFH. Also known as Work From Home, often wearing your boxer shorts or pyjamas.

Conference Calls. Please remember to put on some decent pants and undergarments lest you need to get up in the midst of it and be discovered pants-less.

Socialising. Virtual catch-ups using Facetime (aptly dubbed FaceWine as there was always wine involved), Zoom, WhatsApp video calls. Anything to keep in touch. If all else failed, one could always shout at neighbours within reasonable hearing distance.

Food Delivery. With contactless delivery, just put the food outside your door. I have a designated Ikea stool I leave outside my unit for this purpose, with a note. And so many food options! No one is beyond board now! Even the most expensive restaurant in town offered delivery or take-out services. Oh how the mighty have fallen. Others have joined Facebook's restaurant rescue groups for direct ordering, with free or low-fee delivery.

Waking up late. What was time anyway.

Eating non-stop and putting on weight. This was completely universal. It was actually boredom.

Online Learning. We learnt new skills and everybody became academics with MasterClass, Coursera, Udemy and even some well-known academic institutions. The best use of your spare time, if any.

Music lessons and tuition. All through video calls and modern technology.

Free performances. Watch world class performances online, free-of-charge. The selection included concerts (from Andrea Bocelli to Metallica), musicals (remember when Phantom of the Opera was made free for 48 hours?), opera, ballet, from such institutions some people could only dream of watching live, such as The Met.

And of recent, Tarzan hair and Natural Beauty.

NEW HOBBIES:
Everybody became a runner. The parks used to be empty, now everybody was suddenly an athlete.

Everybody became a park conservator. We were conversant about parks and what were the times to visit, solely for exercise, of course.

Singing. It was *Circuit Breaker Got Talent* as everyone became a singer at home. Once I walked past a row of flats whilst out for essentials and there was this loud competition with Cantonese and Hokkien oldies coming from different blocks.

Some of us opted to become painters. Well, some more successfully so than others.

Everybody became hairdressers. Our mums cutting our hair. Well my mother had always dabbled in hairdressing as a hobby and actually was a rather good one, except, when she made my hair look like a poodle's. Children believe whatever we tell them. I was 10. She told me it looked amazing and I believed her. Now I see my photos from that year, and it's obvious that it was a failed experiment. My mum had sheepishly admitted it.

Birdwatching. Equipped with binoculars for spying on neighbours, or in my case to judge other Covidiots who had not yet turned to the other side (like I did). "They don't wear masks!", "They walked too close!" or "Hey, those two don't live together!" as if everybody was supposed to live in sin so as not to get a ticket.

Cooking and baking. Why did everyone on my Facebook suddenly become chefs? I too tried making muffins from scratch but I burnt them. I'd stick to singing and writing for now. See, when I say, *"Baby, let's go to the kitchen,"* I don't necessarily mean to cook.

Sports instructors and personal trainers. Home exercising with whatever tools were available at home, including your wife. Some people made personal videos on how to keep fit. Let's see how long these inspiring individuals last.

Tic Toc challenge. Oh, please.

Online shopping. Definitely on the rise. I've been buying gadgets these days, necessities for a homebound existence such as mobile phone and laptop holders, seeing as the only way I'd see my friends were on screens.

Netflix. Who didn't.

MariKondo. Spring clean and throw everything! Streamline your life! You might try evaluating your current partner too: touch your partner (if you have one) with both hands and ask yourself if he/she spark joy to your life. And there I was, foreseeing a new horde of singles upon Circuit Breaker being lifted. New opportunities!

Free porn. It did not affect my lifestyle one bit but my male friends were very happy as PornHub could be accessed for free in Singapore too. It couldn't be just the Italians who got it for free. Equal opportunity for all males.

Finally, attending Church in the comfort of your living room. Also free.

Epilogue

The Road Ahead

—

Hello friends!

So here we are, at the final chapter, where the ending is the beginning of our new normal!

What will be the road ahead? It seems to me, at this moment, that nobody knows. Not the experts, not doctors, certainly not POTUS or even the WHO which changes their mind everyday whether we should be wearing a mask or not, or how long this pandemic is going to last.

To be fair, I believe most people are doing the very best they can. This is a deadly plague of such unprecedented global scale that the Millennials have witnessed and lived through.

Faced with such an uncertain future, what must one do?

As I did my research towards wrapping up this delightful project, in the absence of a proverbial crystal ball, I had to do some manual labour, i.e. ask around and put on my own thinking cap. The one theme everyone unitedly agreed on as absolutely vital for us going ahead is: adaptability.

"Accept our reality, adapt and reinvent ourselves for the new landscape." The species that adapts, survives. The same goes for phones or dinosaurs.

There are many things we wish could have happened. We wish we had been kinder to nature, we wish people had less adventurous food choices, we wish we are all less profit seeking and more people-focus, we wish, we wish and we wish. But as the Italian saying goes: "*Che successe, successe.*" Simply put, 'what happened, happened.'

Assigning blame and complaining will not help us move forward. Even more so than ever, we need to work together to overcome the severe inconvenience the disease has caused us all. Top of mind for many, is the anxiety over our affected livelihoods. Other than those in the funeral business, I struggle to think who on this planet is not adversely affected by this wretched virus.

In the spirit of adapting and surviving, let us look with an open mind for new opportunities and for ingenious alternatives 'outside the box'. We had no choice but to survive, and survive well we will. The human race has survived many plagues prior to this. This too shall pass.

Whilst in the spirit of 'Life is Short', short of doing my very own bucket list, my personal recommendations are as follows.

The time to do the goals that we had put off is <u>NOW</u>. Take the risk and imagine that we can not fail. What's the worse that can happen? Explore our other talents. Other than that, gratitude and forgiveness help. Finally, be less concerned about what people think or say about us. Remain unapologetically you.

On humour. The truths of the world can always be seen from the side of humour. This is especially so in the face of adversity. The world need not be darker than it is.

On morality. Whatever compass of morality, belief or spirituality we choose, let it be one that makes us a better person, on earth as it is in Heaven.

On love. I have observed that only by giving love will we receive it back in return. It strangely comes back to us from other sources! Somehow that is how the Universe works. Hence the next point.

On paying it forward. There will never be a better time to extend a helping hand to others. Those who have more are tasked with giving more to others in need. We can all start from a grassroots level, and together we'll make a difference.

I hope that when people read this account one day, when the pandemic is but a distant memory, the humour and our survival stories remain.

Thank you for choosing this book and being a part of *Diary of a Former Covidiot.* I sincerely hope you were entertained.

Let us look forward to discovering what surprises life has in store for each of us along the way. My very best wishes for the journey ahead, may your life be full of joy, no matter what.

With love,

Christina

Acknowledgements

—

Melvin Neo, my fabulous editor: thank you for believing in me. Felix Cheong, my mentor and friend; and Eleanor O'Connor, another dear friend, for all your invaluable inputs.

Thanking my family and the following individuals for their support and contributions (by first name alphabetical order):

Ae Ree Jeong, Alex Fain, Alfani Cahya, Alvin Chua, Andre Surya, Ben Chan, Bernie Guan, Brian Tan, Christina Hindle, Clarissa Santoso, Daniel Chua, Dedo Liang, Dominique Boer, Edwin Orlando Cruz, Ethel Reyes, Fan Zhang, Fiona Wilson, Gabrielle Loh, Gwenyth Wee, Husnul Khotimah, Hye Jin Lee, Jack Lin, Jolanta Nagajek, Jonathan Lukman, Kelvin Chia, Ling Ong, Lawrence Koh, Lyn Lyn Tang, Mark Jong, Melody Chong, Michael Tay, Nguyen Tung Lam, Peter Ng, Rangga Winantyo, Rannie Owyong, Reuben Lai, Ronnie Wee, Samet Gogus, Shanti Bhattacharya, Shawn Peh, Sheryl Ho, Shiyu Ching, Steph Gwen Koh, Stephen Kim, Steve Aw, Steven Ang, Ting Ting Lu, Tse Yi Lam, Zhuo Neng Goh.

About the Author

—

Christina and her family have called Singapore home for over two decades. Born in Indonesia, she subsequently went on to experience life in several other countries including Australia and the UK, and merrily collected four degrees along the way; half for herself, half for her beloved parents.

As an amiable observer of people, she finds human nature fascinating and a great source of inspiration.

As a soprano she trained at the Royal Academy of Music in London and has enjoyed singing at the Carnegie Hall in New York.

Today, Christina regularly appears in Singapore's opera scene and writes humorous realistic fiction while leading life as a modern single mother.